Guide to the Implementation and Auditing of ISMS Controls Based on ISO/IEC 27001

Guide to the Implementation and Auditing of ISMS Controls Based on ISO/IEC 27001

Bridget Kenyon and Edward (Ted) Humphreys

bsi.

First published in the UK in 1999
Second edition 2002
Third edition 2005
Fourth edition 2014

by
BSI Standards Limited
389 Chiswick High Road
London W4 4AL

Typeset in Great Britain by Letterpart Limited, www.letterpart.com
Printed in Great Britain by Berforts Group, www.berforts.co.uk

British Library Cataloguing in Publication Data
A catalogue record for this book is available from the British Library

ISBN 978-0-580-82910-9

Contents

Information Security Management Systems Guidance series

The Information Security Management Systems (ISMS) series of books is designed to provide users with assistance on establishing, implementing, maintaining, checking and auditing their ISMS in order to prepare for certification. Titles in this Information Security Management Systems Guidance series include:

- *Guidelines on requirements and preparation for ISMS certification based on ISO/IEC 27001* (ref.: BIP 0071);
- *Are you ready for an ISMS audit based on ISO/IEC 27001?* (ref.: BIP 0072);
- *Guide to the implementation and auditing of ISMS controls based on ISO/IEC 27001* (ref.: BIP 0073);
- *Measuring the effectiveness of your ISMS implementations based on ISO/IEC 27001* (ref.: BIP 0074);
- *Information security risk management — Handbook for ISO/IEC 27001* (ref.: BIP 0076).

Foreword

Information is one of your organization's most valuable assets. The objectives of information security are to protect the confidentiality, integrity and availability of information. These basic elements of information security help to ensure that an organization can protect against:

- sensitive or confidential information being given away, leaked or disclosed, both accidentally or in an unauthorized way;
- personally identifiable information being compromised;
- critical information being accidentally or intentionally modified without your knowledge;
- any important business information being lost without trace or hope of recovery;
- any important business information being rendered unavailable when needed.

It should be the responsibility of all managers, information system owners or custodians, and users in general, to ensure that their information is properly managed and protected from the variety of risks and threats faced by every organization. The two standards, ISO/IEC 27001:2013, *Information technology — Security techniques — Information security management systems — Requirements* and ISO/IEC 27002:2013, *Information technology — Security techniques – Code of practice for information security controls*, together provide a basis for organizations to develop an effective information security management framework for managing and protecting their important business assets, whilst minimizing their risks, maximizing the investments and business opportunities of their organizations, and ensuring their information systems continue to be available and operational.

ISO/IEC 27001:2013 is the requirements standard that can be used for accredited third-party information security management system (ISMS) certifications. Organizations going through the accredited certification route to obtain an ISMS certificate would need their ISMS to be audited and assessed by an accredited certification body to ensure that they have appropriate management processes and systems in place that conform to the requirements specified in the ISO/IEC 27001 ISMS standard.

ISO/IEC 27002:2013, *Information technology — Security techniques — Code of practice for information security controls* provides a

---

comprehensive set of best practice controls for information security and implementation guidance. Organizations can adopt these controls as part of the risk treatment process specified in ISO/IEC 27001:2013 in order to manage the risks they face to their information assets.

This guide, BIP 0073, as with the other guides in the BIP 0070 series, is designed to provide users with assistance in establishing, implementing and maintaining their ISMS to help them in preparing for ISMS certification. This is the fourth edition of this guide and it has been produced to reflect the publication of the new editions of ISO/IEC 27001 and ISO/IEC 27002.

Note: A document such as this is provided with the best of intentions. It reflects publicly available common best practice that is derived by a consensus among international experts with a wide variety of skills, knowledge and experience in the subject. This guide makes no claim to be exhaustive or definitive and users of this guide may need to seek further guidance in implementing the requirements of ISO/IEC 27001:2013 or in using the guidance found in ISO/IEC 27002:2013. Furthermore, there will always be other aspects where additional guidance is required relevant to the organizational, operational, legal and environmental context of the business, including specific threats, controls, regulatory compliance, governance and good practice. BSI or the authors of this guide cannot be held liable by organizations, users or third parties for the execution or implementation of this information. It has been assumed in the drafting of the information and advice given in this guide that the execution of this information by organizations and users is entrusted to appropriately qualified and experienced people.

1 General

1.1 Scope of this guide

This document provides guidance on the implementation of information security management system (ISMS) control requirements and on auditing existing control implementations to help organizations preparing for certification in accordance with ISO/IEC 27001:2013.

The contents of this guide include the ISMS control requirements that should be addressed by organizations considering certification. Section 2 of this guide discusses each of the controls in Annex A of ISO/IEC 27001:2013 from two different viewpoints:

1. implementation guidance – describing what needs to be considered to fulfil the control requirements when implementing the controls from ISO/IEC 27001:2013, Annex A. This guidance is aligned with ISO/IEC 27002:2013, which gives advice on the implementation of the controls;
2. auditing guidance – describing what should be checked when examining the implementation of ISO/IEC 27001:2013 controls to ensure that the implementation covers the essential ISMS control requirements.

It is important to emphasize that this guide does not cover the implementation or auditing of the ISMS process requirements; these are covered in BIP 0071. These are also discussed in more detail in 1.3, 'Meeting ISO/IEC 27001 requirements'.

1.2 Field of application

1.2.1 Usage

This guide is intended to be used by those involved in:

*   designing, implementing and/or maintaining an ISMS;
*   preparing for ISMS audits and assessments;

- undertaking both internal and third-party ISMS audits and assessments.[1]

This guide makes reference to the following standards:

- ISO/IEC 27001:2013 – the requirements specification for an ISMS. This standard is used as the basis for accredited certification;
- ISO/IEC 27002:2013 – a reference for selecting controls as part of the implementation of an ISMS, and a guidance document for organizations implementing commonly accepted security controls.

This guide will be updated following any changes to these standards. Organizations should therefore ensure that the correct version is being used for compliance checks related to pre-certification, certification and post-certification purposes.

1.2.2 Compliance

To claim compliance with the requirements in ISO/IEC 27001:2013, the organization needs to demonstrate that it has all the processes in place and needs to provide appropriate objective evidence to support such claims. Any exclusion of controls found to be necessary to satisfy the risk acceptance criteria needs to be justified and evidence needs to be provided that the associated risks have been knowingly and objectively accepted by those in management who have the executive responsibility for making such decisions and who are accountable for making such decisions.

Excluding any of the requirements specified in ISO/IEC 27001:2013, Clauses 4 to 10 is not acceptable.[2]

The implementation of a set of ISMS processes results in the organization deploying a system of controls based on a risk management approach to manage its risks. The organization should have implemented an effective system of management controls and processes as part of its ISMS, and it should be able to demonstrate this by providing evidence to the ISMS auditor (whether it be a first-, second- or third-party audit).

This guide can be used by those who may not have an immediate need for an audit, but who require a specification for establishing and implementing an ISMS based on industry-accepted best practice processes. However, claiming compliance with ISO/IEC 27001:2013 does require the organization to have at least an internal ISMS audit in place whether or not it goes for a third-party audit at a later stage. The

---

[1] Auditors deployed by the organization to carry out an internal ISMS audit, auditors from certification bodies and assessors from accreditation bodies engaged in assessing certification bodies.
[2] See ISO/IEC 27001:2013, Clause 1.

organization may not have a business case for a third-party audit, but, to be compliant with ISO/IEC 27001:2013, the internal ISMS audit is mandatory. This guide can, of course, also be used by those preparing for a second- and third-party audit.

1.3 Meeting ISO/IEC 27001 requirements

There are two different types of requirements stated in ISO/IEC 27001:2013:

1. the requirements contained in the ISMS process that are described in ISO/IEC 27001:2013, Clauses 4 to 10;
2. the ISMS controls contained in ISO/IEC 27001:2013, Annex A.

The ISMS process requirements address how an organization should establish and maintain its ISMS. An organization that wants to achieve ISO/IEC 27001:2013 certification needs to comply with all these requirements – exclusions are not acceptable. The guide BIP 0071, *Guidelines on requirements and preparation for ISMS certification based on ISO/IEC 27001* provides guidance on the ISMS process requirements and certification process, and preparing for certification. An organization can also check whether it has implemented all of the ISMS process requirements by using the checklists provided by the guide BIP 0072, *Are you ready for an ISMS audit based on ISO/IEC 27001?*

1.4 General

The ISMS control requirements stated in ISO/IEC 27001:2013, Annex A are applicable for an organization unless the risk assessment and the risk acceptance criteria prove that this is not the case. This is stated in ISO/IEC 27001: 'The organization shall...produce a Statement of Applicability that contains the necessary controls...and justification for inclusions, whether they are implemented or not, and the justification for exclusions of controls from Annex A' (ISO/IEC 27001, 6.1.3).

2 Implementing and auditing ISMS control objectives and controls

In this section, each of the control objectives and control requirements identified in ISO/IEC 27001:2013, Annex A as requirements of the certification scheme are discussed from implementation and auditing viewpoints. These take into account the implementation advice given in ISO/IEC 27002:2013, the code of practice for information security controls. The complete control objectives from ISO/IEC 27001:2013 are included in this document to clarify the requirements.

2.1 Information security policies (ISO/IEC 27001:2013, Clause A.5)

2.1.1 Management direction for information security (ISO/IEC 27001:2013, A.5.1)

Objective: To provide management direction and support for information security in accordance with business requirements and relevant laws and regulations.

2.1.1.1 Policies for information security (ISO/IEC 27001:2013, A.5.1.1)

'A set of policies for information security shall be defined, approved by management, published and communicated to employees and relevant external parties.'

Implementation guidance

Guidance on what an information security policy should contain can be found in ISO/IEC 27002:2013, 5.1.1. Organizational policies should be simple and to the point. It might not be appropriate to combine every level of policy into one document, and the top-level information security policy can easily make reference to more detailed policies, e.g. using hyperlinks. Indeed, the top-level policy should normally be capable of expression within a single piece of paper. It might also be part of a more general policy document. The information security policy should be distributed and communicated to all staff, and to all relevant external parties, e.g. others regularly working on the organization's premises.

When the information security policy is distributed outside the organization, it should be unclassified; any sensitive information that might have been contained in it should be removed prior to such distribution.

The appropriate lower-level policies should be available to staff as needed, dependent on the job function and the associated security requirements, and classified accordingly. The information security policy and several or all of the lower-level policies might be contained within a security policy manual.

The information security policies should be subject to version control, and should be part of the ISMS documentation. It should be ensured that all those with responsibilities for information security have access to all necessary policies, and the information security policies should also be made available to anyone with appropriate authorization on request.

Auditing guidance

The information security policy does not need to be extensive, but should clearly state senior management's commitment to information security, be under change and version control and be signed by the appropriate senior manager. The policy should at least address the following topics:

- a definition of information security, its overall scope and objectives;
- reasons why information security is important to the organization;
- management support for information security;
- a framework for risk assessment and risk management, and for selecting control objectives and controls;
- a brief summary of the security policies, principles, standards and compliance requirements;
- definition of all relevant information security responsibilities (see also 2.2.1.1 below);
- reference to supporting documentation, e.g. more detailed policies;
- how non-compliances and exceptions will be handled.

The auditor should confirm that the policy is readily accessible to all employees and all relevant external parties, and that the policy is communicated to all relevant persons, checking that they are aware of its existence and understand its contents. The policy may be a stand-alone statement or part of more extensive documentation (e.g. a security policy manual) that defines how the information security policy is implemented in the organization. In general, most, if not all, employees covered by the ISMS scope will have some responsibilities for information security, and auditors should review any declarations to the contrary with care.

The auditor should also confirm that the policy has an owner who is responsible for its maintenance (see also 2.1.1.2) and that it is updated appropriately following any changes affecting the information security requirements of the organization, such as changes in the original risk assessment.

Topic-specific policies that underpin the top-level policy should be clearly linked to the needs of their target group(s) and cover all topics that are necessary to provide a foundation for other security controls.

2.1.1.2 Review of the policies for information security (ISO/IEC 27001:2013, A.5.1.2)

'The policies for information security shall be reviewed at planned intervals or if significant changes occur to ensure their continuing suitability, adequacy and effectiveness.'

Implementation guidance

This control forms an important part of the continuous maintenance, review and updating of the ISMS that is also addressed in Clause 9 of ISO/IEC 27001:2013, 'Performance evaluation'. This maintenance process should be responsive to all security-relevant changes related to the ISMS. Scheduled periodic reviews and defined review procedures are essential to keep the information security policy document current and to ensure that it accurately reflects how the organization is managing its risks. Appointing an owner of the information security policy with responsibility for its review helps to ensure that the review does actually take place.

Auditing guidance

This control is necessary to ensure that the information security policies are current and effective. The policies play an important role in the establishment and maintenance of an ISMS. Auditors should confirm that the organization has appointed an owner for the information security policy with responsibility for its review or, if this has not taken place, ensured that other clear responsibilities are in place for the review. Auditors should also confirm that the organization has developed procedures to react to any incidents, new vulnerabilities or threats, changes in technology, or anything else that is related to the ISMS that might make a review of the policy necessary. In addition, there should be scheduled periodic reviews to ensure that the policy remains appropriate and is cost-effective to implement in relation to the protection achieved. The auditor should confirm that the time schedule for such reviews is appropriate for the overall risk situation. Auditors should also check the organization's plans for distributing updated policies and verify that all employees are made aware of the changes.

2.2 Organization of information security (ISO/IEC 27001:2013, Clause A.6)

2.2.1 Internal organization (ISO/IEC 27001:2013, A.6.1)

Objective: To establish a management framework to initiate and control the implementation and operation of information security within the organization.

2.2.1.1 Information security roles and responsibilities (ISO/IEC 27001:2013, A.6.1.1)

'All information security responsibilities shall be defined and allocated.'

Implementation guidance

The organization will be vulnerable to widespread insecurity if employees, contractors and third-party users are not aware of the information security policy, what they have to comply with and what is expected of them. For all employees, contractors and third-party users, roles and responsibilities should be defined and clearly communicated, in line with the organization's security policies.

Responsibility for the protection of individual assets and for carrying out specific security processes should be clearly defined and documented in accordance with the information security policies (see 2.5.1.1). This is not a trivial task and should encompass every employee. It is fundamental that management and staff should be told what is expected of them, especially where information security is not generally likely to be their first interest. In general, all staff should have a basic responsibility for security noted in their job description (see also 2.3.1.2), and they should understand their security responsibilities to be an integral part of their job function. Those employees, contractors and third-party users with substantial and complex security responsibilities should have these detailed in a document, e.g. in the job description or in the terms and conditions of employment (see 2.3.1.2). This document could be signed by the employees, contractors and third-party users, and their manager, to indicate acceptance and understanding. All employees, contractors and third-party users should be given a personal copy.

Information security responsibilities may also be delegated to others during work processes. In such cases, it is important that the persons delegating their responsibilities are aware that they remain responsible, and that it is part of their tasks to determine that any delegated tasks and responsibilities have been performed correctly.

Auditing guidance

Auditors should confirm that somebody with overall responsibility for information security has been appointed (e.g. an information security manager).

The information security policy, and/or the risk treatment plan, is normally used to define the higher-level responsibilities and reporting structure, but the explicit detail of information security responsibilities would normally be contained in job descriptions or some other format based on the individual. All employees having specific roles and responsibilities for information security should have a document, e.g. the job description, that defines these security roles and responsibilities. Auditors should check that this is available, and that the employee is fully aware of their roles and responsibilities. One way of demonstrating this is to check whether the document has been signed by both the employee and the appropriate manager to signify understanding and acceptance. Another aspect for the auditor to check is the date of the document, and whether it contains correct and consistent details relating to information security functions. A check of the security responsibilities defined in policy statements and individual procedures should provide full consistency with the individual roles and responsibilities.

Organizations might vary in where the documents describing the roles and responsibilities are held; some will be with the individual, others with personnel departments. In the latter case, it should be checked that the individual has access to this information – they should have their own copy, as a person is unlikely to comply with a document last seen perhaps up to a year ago. Where individuals have jobs with specific security requirements, such as a network administrator, ensure that the job description or an additional document fully reflects this – statements covering all employees are not acceptable in such cases. Auditors should confirm that all documentation of this nature is current and properly controlled.

It is particularly important that new personnel in jobs fully understand their responsibilities and the paperwork should be completed at the time of appointment, not at the next convenient review. Auditors should pay particular attention to temporary employees, contractors and third-party users. The same rules should apply for them; exceptions are not acceptable. There should be descriptions of security roles and responsibilities for everyone working within the scope of the ISMS.

The clear definition and allocation of information security roles and responsibilities should be carefully investigated, as this can be a potential weak link in many situations.

2.2.1.2 Segregation of duties (ISO/IEC 27001:2013, A.6.1.2)

'Conflicting duties and areas of responsibility shall be segregated to reduce opportunities for unauthorized or unintentional modification or misuse of the organization's assets.'

Implementation guidance

Segregation of duties is a traditional business control used to reduce vulnerability to staff errors and misuse of all kinds. While most of the people employed in an organization are essentially honest, there might be some who are not. A greater number of people might become negligent if their activities are not controlled. This can lead to problems with integrity (people as well as information), loss of confidentiality and resources being unavailable for their proper purpose. Ensure that risk assessment properly identifies the risks of unsegregated activities.

Dividing the job up between two or more staff provides a check at the point of handover where one person can see that another has done what they are supposed to have done. In sensitive areas, for example, the use of two keys or passwords by separate staff ensures that no one obtains access to a resource without a second person either authorizing or confirming an authority.

Many frauds and accounting deceptions are committed by people who have been given access to too many functions within an accounting system and/or do not need separate authorization for their activities. A well-known disaster of this type was the Barings Bank losses, which resulted in the collapse of the entire business. Segregation prevents staff from operating on their own to create such incidents. Although the possibility of collusion remains, it is very rare that more than two will take the personal risk.

In small organizations, where segregation can be difficult to implement, the principle should be applied as far as possible, with additional controls, such as increased monitoring, being implemented to compensate for any lack of segregation. If segregation of duties cannot be achieved, it can at least help to record all activities and to have procedures in place for independent review of these records to identify any suspicious or unauthorized activity.

Auditing guidance

As noted in ISO/IEC 27002:2013, 6.1.2, small organizations might find it difficult to implement this control. This may be due to a lack of resources. At least for critical roles, some provisions should be in place – if nothing else is possible, at least crucial activities should be logged and the logs reviewed. The auditor should ask to see these logs, and ask for evidence of the review process. For larger organizations, this principle should be an established fact and properly demonstrated in their procedures. Of those procedures which should be considered for independent operations, security administration and audit are possibly the most critical and should be considered first.

The auditor should look at what independent verification of data and results is done between processing stages or before release. As part of its risk assessment, the organization should have considered critical processes and whether any one person is responsible for carrying out too many of the checks and balances. Look at work arrangements for critical tasks: how are periods of sickness or holidays covered? Does this compromise independence? The organization might need to enforce mandatory holiday periods to achieve effective segregation.

2.2.1.3 Contact with authorities (ISO/IEC 27001:2013, A.6.1.3)

'Appropriate contacts with relevant authorities shall be maintained.'

Implementation guidance

The organization should have procedures in place to identify and establish that all appropriate liaisons are in place with external regulatory bodies, service providers and any other organization important for information security. In addition, the necessary approvals, reporting procedures and formats should be agreed to ensure that all relevant information can be exchanged.

It might be helpful to establish the function of a liaison officer responsible for contacting authorities. This person can also receive information from the authorities that might be helpful to guard against certain events, and to prepare for upcoming new legislation or regulations.

Auditing guidance

This control requires appropriate liaisons to be in place with external regulatory bodies, service providers and others that may have a crucial role in either preventing security incidents or mitigating their effects. The auditor should therefore look for evidence regarding the existence of the necessary contacts in business continuity and contingency plans, and infrastructure support documents. The auditor should also look for evidence that legal, industrial, operational and technical requirements are being monitored for conformity as appropriate. The auditor should ensure that the organization is able to demonstrate that it knows and has documented all applicable legal requirements, and that all contacts necessary to conform to these requirements are in place. Agreements and approvals should also be reviewed by the auditor to ensure that information being provided to relevant authorities is suitable and authorized.

2.2.1.4 Contact with special interest groups (ISO/IEC 27001:2013, A.6.1.4)

'Appropriate contacts with special interest groups or other specialist security forums and professional associations shall be maintained.'

Implementation guidance

Good ideas can be acquired from a meeting of security managers of other organizations, many of whom have long and valuable experience in the subject, as well as from joining specialist groups, standards committees, etc. While some involve a membership fee, they will usually give you a taste of what they have to offer before you make up your mind. Other bodies do not have members as such but are useful sources of information; many of them communicate via the internet, which can be a useful source of security information. Try a search on a keyword or organization using one of the many search tools available.

Exchanges of security information should be controlled to ensure that confidential information is not passed to unauthorized persons. Some bodies operate on a strict non-disclosure basis to enable confidential discussion.

Auditing guidance

It might be helpful for an organization to participate in discussions on best practice and share knowledge on threats being promulgated across the industry. A large organization can be involved in security specialist groups, standards committees or similar activities outside its own environment. Smaller organizations are unlikely to be able to support extensive involvement but attendance at appropriate conferences and seminars would partly address this. In either case, auditors should check that procedures are in place to share and distribute any information received from such participation within the organization in the most beneficial way. These procedures should also address that no confidential information is exchanged without proper authorization.

2.2.1.5 Information security in project management (ISO/IEC 27001:2013, A.6.1.5)

'Information security shall be addressed in project management, regardless of the type of the project.'

Implementation guidance

Projects are a major component of any organization's work, at any time. Inappropriately controlled security during the delivery of a project risks exposing the organization to uncontrolled business risks, resulting in security incidents. Equally, the products and services that the project intends to deliver must also be suitably secure. A product that is capable of doing what its customer asks for, but which also provides a route for

---

compromise of an environment is not fit for purpose and should be unlikely if security is fully integrated into project delivery.

In order to ensure that a project preserves security during its lifespan, and produces secure deliverables, two risk assessments should be carried out at the start of the project. One risk assessment should consider risks relating to the activities of the project itself, and the other should cover risks relating to the deliverable(s). Information security requirements should be considered to be part of the operational requirements of the project. These should be prioritized according to the risk that the controls are intended to counter.

Care should be taken to distinguish between the concept of 'project risk' and information security risk: the project may have a risk register, which lists risks to the delivery of the project, but this may not be a suitable vehicle within which to record and manage information security risk. Consider having an information security risk register, which integrates with the organization's ISMS and is therefore less subject to the drivers that can overwhelm local project requirements. A project may choose to remove requirements to improve its chances of delivering on time; proposals for changes to information security controls should be raised to the appropriate organizational level so that the risk to the organization may be managed suitably.

Since projects inevitably change during their lifespans, information security should be re-assessed as part of any project change process, to ensure that risk mitigations are still suitable. There should also be consideration of information security at all key stages in the project's lifespan.

Finally, the transition phase of deliverables should be very carefully managed to ensure that project security requirements are mirrored in the deliverables that survive the project.

Auditing guidance

The auditor should first check the documentation for the project methodology in use, and check that it contains a requirement for identification of information security objectives, risks (as distinct from project risks) and controls. The methodology should also contain checkpoints throughout the project life cycle to ensure that information security is addressed regularly. Any deviations in the project should automatically initiate a review of existing information security risk assessment work, to ascertain whether it needs to be revised and changes made to existing controls, new controls added, and/or controls removed. There should be a statement that responsibilities for information security must be defined and associated with particular roles.

In terms of what should be documented for each project, the auditor should look for evidence that there is a record of information security objectives and a risk assessment for each project. Evidence should also be obtained to show that information security risks can be associated with controls. Responsibilities for information security during each phase of the project should be defined, and roles should be associated with these responsibilities.

2.2.2 Mobile devices and teleworking (ISO/IEC 27001:2013, A.6.2)

Objective: To ensure the security of teleworking and use of mobile devices.

2.2.2.1 Mobile device policy (ISO/IEC 27001:2013, A.6.2.1)

'A policy and supporting security measures shall be adopted to manage the risks introduced by using mobile devices.'

Implementation guidance

In most cases, the use of mobile computing and communication facilities takes place outside the organization, e.g. in airports, and on planes or trains, when travelling; during conferences and meetings; or with customers at their organization or home. There are many additional risks to mobile equipment that result from this way of working.

Employees using mobile equipment should be aware of these risks and should adapt their behaviour accordingly. The organization should develop a mobile computing policy describing the controls that should be in place, and employees should only be allowed to use mobile computing facilities after they receive the policy and sufficient training and awareness education.

Other security risks when using mobile computing facilities are related to information exchange. Backups should be made regularly, and effective and frequently updated virus protection should be used if any information transfer takes place. In the case of remote connections to the organization's site, authentication not only for the machine but also for the authorized user should be in place, to avoid such connections being exploited, e.g. by somebody who has stolen a laptop.

ISO/IEC 27002:2013 describes in 6.2.1 a number of controls that can be applied to protect information and facilities used in mobile computing and communications.

Auditing guidance

The auditor should confirm that the use of all mobile computing and communication devices and equipment has been identified by the organization. This includes the use of mobile phones, and the use of laptops, notebooks or palmtops, outside the organization's premises (e.g. at home, at customer sites, in hotels, during travel or at conference venues), and any remote connections to the organization's internal information processing facilities using such devices. Since such devices and equipment are generally used and mobile computing and communication activities tend to take place outside the organization, their use will normally be difficult to audit directly.

It is therefore particularly important that the auditor looks closely at the controls, rules and procedures that the organization has in place to ensure that such devices are used in a secure way. This includes the controls that should be implemented to protect such devices. User training and awareness, authorization processes and security arrangements for using such devices should be in place, as described in ISO/IEC 27002:2013, 6.2.1.

As is feasible, audit evidence should be collected to check that all these controls are implemented correctly. Also, audit checks for controls should include what the policy says about password and virus protection on mobile computers. Check that there are sufficient controls in place to secure remote access, and that cryptographic controls are applied where necessary.

2.2.2.2 Teleworking (ISO/IEC 27001:2013, A.6.2.2)

'A policy and supporting security measures shall be implemented to protect information accessed, processed or stored at teleworking sites.'

Implementation guidance

As in the mobile computing environment, the main security problems with teleworking arise from the location where this work is taking place. The employee's home does not normally have the same level of physical security, and the work area is often easily accessible by family members and visitors. In order to reduce these risks, teleworking should only take place after the organization has developed appropriate policies and procedures, has put in place physical controls to secure the work area and has raised the awareness of the employee doing teleworking sufficiently to control the physical and logical access to the information processing facilities used for the teleworking activities.

The connections between the organization's site and the teleworking facilities should be secured to ensure that information cannot be destroyed, damaged, compromised or modified, and the information that is accessible remotely should be restricted to a minimum.

ISO/IEC 27002:2013, 6.2.2 contains a detailed list of actions the organization should consider prior to authorizing any teleworking activities.

Auditing guidance

Teleworking activities should only be authorized if sufficient controls are in place, including physical controls, access control and the security of the remote connection. The homeworking equipment should be included in the asset register. There should be some mechanism for establishing and controlling what information is transmitted to and from, and used at, home or other teleworking environment.

There should be some defined policy on the use of the equipment for other activities, such as games software and accessing the internet, any of which can introduce problems when allowed to interfere with sensitive data. Check that the controls in ISO/IEC 27002:2013, 6.2.2 are implemented to sufficiently secure the teleworking environment. The auditor needs to confirm that, if the organization is using teleworking arrangements, there are sufficient controls in place in consideration of the above.

2.3 Human resource security (ISO/IEC 27001:2013, Clause A.7)

2.3.1 Prior to employment (ISO/IEC 27001:2013, A.7.1)

Objective: To ensure that employees and contractors understand their responsibilities and are suitable for the roles for which they are considered.

2.3.1.1 Screening (ISO/IEC 27001:2013, A.7.1.1)

'Background verification checks on all candidates for employment shall be carried out in accordance with relevant laws, regulations and ethics and shall be proportional to the business requirements, the classification of the information to be accessed and the perceived risks.'

Implementation guidance

Screening is the essential control that can prevent the organization employing the wrong person. Legal restraints may put a limit on the checks that the organization may consider. Whatever screening and data collection takes place, care should be taken that all applicable legislation and regulations are complied with. Identification checks, CV reviews, and checks of qualifications and character references should be made. Where the proposed position provides access to sensitive, critical and/or personally identifiable information, it is essential to get to the details of the applicant's responsibilities in previous positions and get them confirmed by previous employers. While one should be wary of very cursory references, remember that some organizations will not, as a matter of policy, offer any detail or opinion other than confirmation of the period employed and the last position held. Gaps or irregularities in employment should be questioned.

All exchanges and interviews should be fully documented and retained on file throughout employment and for a reasonable period after it ceases, or after rejection of an application pending any possible appeal by the applicant. The required screening processes should take place for all people working within the scope of the ISMS, irrespective of whether they are employees, contractors or third-party users.

Auditing guidance

The auditor needs to collect relevant evidence that screening procedures for personnel recruitment (including contractors, third-party users and temporary staff) are being enforced and include procedures for appropriate verification checks. ISO/IEC 27002:2013, 7.1.1 lists items to be covered. In particular, organizations should not rely solely on employee-supplied CVs or qualifications without suitable verification of the claims made. The auditor needs to check any follow-up actions, such as conversations with referees, are documented. It should be checked that managers are aware of their responsibilities for evaluating and reviewing the work carried out in their area of responsibility, including all related security responsibilities. The auditor should also check that all information related to personnel verification checks is handled in accordance with all relevant regulations and legislation (e.g. data protection).

2.3.1.2 Terms and conditions of employment (ISO/IEC 27001:2013, A.7.1.2)

'The contractual agreements with employees and contractors shall state their and the organization's responsibilities for information security.'

Implementation guidance

It is important that employees, contractors and third-party users are aware of their security and legal responsibilities regarding the handling of information and the classifications and use of information processing facilities, and the consequences of not complying with security or legal requirements. This also extends to any contractual obligations that the organization has entered into and that might relate to the employee's, contractor's or third-party user's scope of work. Any such responsibilities should be included in any terms and conditions of employment.

It is also important that employees, contractors and third-party users sign a confidentiality agreement (see also 2.9.2.4) before starting their work, and that they understand that such responsibilities may extend beyond their normal working environment and working hours, as well as applying to home working, working on customers' sites and any other form of remote working.

In addition, the organization's responsibilities for handling personal data of employees, contractors and third-party users should be stated, e.g. compliance with data protection legislation (see also 2.14.1.4).

Auditing guidance

Auditors should check whether the terms and conditions of employment accurately describe both the employer's and the employee's, contractor's or third-party user's responsibilities for information security. These descriptions should cover all security-relevant aspects of the employee's job, including: responsibilities applicable to legal requirements; responsibilities related to classified information, working outside the organization or outside normal working hours; and those responsibilities that might extend beyond the employee's contract. The terms and conditions should also describe the action that will be taken if employees do not fulfil their security responsibilities. The auditor should check that agreement to, and signing of, the terms and conditions of employment is a necessary requirement before any work starts. The employees, contractors and third-party users should also be required to sign a confidentiality agreement (see also 2.9.2.4) before accessing any confidential information. The auditor should confirm that procedures are in place to ensure that the terms and conditions of employment are updated if the employee's security responsibilities change in any way, e.g. taking on new roles or using new or different information processing facilities.

The auditor should also check that the organization's responsibilities for handling personal data are clearly stated, e.g. compliance with data protection legislation (see also 2.14.1.4).

2.3.2 During employment (ISO/IEC 27001:2013, A.7.2)

Objective: To ensure that employees and contractors are aware of and fulfil their information security responsibilities.

2.3.2.1 Management responsibilities (ISO/IEC 27001:2013, A.7.2.1)

'Management shall require all employees and contractors to apply information security in accordance with the established policies and procedures of the organization.'

Implementation guidance

A key success factor to all security programmes is the support from management, and part of this support is that management is aware of its duty to ensure that everybody in their area of responsibility is acting in compliance with the established policies and procedures, and implemented controls. A list of typical management responsibilities is given in the implementation guidance of ISO/IEC 27002:2013, 7.2.1. An important part of these responsibilities, in addition to the usual management functions, is to give employees, contractors and third-party users the feeling that their information security activities are appreciated, and are as important as other elements of their job function. Another important aspect is to execute the control function and check the compliance with controls, policies and procedures in the day-to-day work situation. This might not need complicated policing exercises – if management is aware of the correct application of controls, policies and procedures, it will easily detect if people in their area of responsibility do not do so.

Auditing guidance

The first thing auditors should check is that managers are aware of their responsibilities, and understand their duty to ensure that employees, contractors and third-party users comply with controls, policies and procedures. The next step is to look for evidence that managers take this responsibility seriously – there could be several indications, such as mentioning information security in meeting agendas, or the reaction of the employees when being asked about management action regarding information security. Awareness evaluations are also encouraging indicators.

It could also help to complete the picture to ask about training programmes for employees, contractors or third-party users who management has identified as not complying with controls, policies or procedures, and what initiates such programmes. Another topic is what management does to motivate its personnel, whether there are reward programmes for good suggestions, or other ways of actively encouraging personnel to support information security.

2.3.2.2 Information security awareness, education and training (ISO/IEC 27001:2013, A.7.2.2)

'All employees of the organization and, where relevant, contractors shall receive appropriate awareness education and training and regular updates in organizational policies and procedures, as relevant for their job function.'

Implementation guidance

The organization is vulnerable to the activities of untrained employees, contractors and third-party users. There is a risk of them producing incorrect and corrupted information or losing it completely. Untrained personnel can take wrong actions and make mistakes through ignorance.

All personnel should be trained in the relevant policies and procedures, including security requirements and other business controls. They should also be trained to use all the IT products and packages required of their position, as well as the relevant security procedures.

Training might be required at one or two levels:

1. Security awareness: every employee and, where relevant, contractor and third-party user should be given the basic level of security awareness training. A course should convey to them the organization's security policy, objectives and framework within which they are expected to work. Essential procedures should be provided and described. Awareness should be refreshed as necessary and through ongoing action.
2. Technical training: those staff with special responsibilities for security (not only security officers) should be provided with the necessary skills. A training plan should be developed for each individual according to the specific knowledge and skill required for the position held. Staff's general development of security knowledge can benefit if they attend suitable conferences. All training, and relevant conference attendance, should be recorded in the individual's training record. Training should be available to employees, agency staff and third-party users, as appropriate. Ensure that training suppliers use appropriately qualified staff and that the syllabus is clear and consistent with the organization's requirements.

Auditing guidance

This control is applicable to all employees, including users of information processing facilities, such as system administrators, managers and application users, as well as senior management and those processing any form of information (e.g. paper based and/or by telephone). It is also applicable to contractors and third-party users, and anyone else having access to information or services within the ISMS.

The first point to note is the appropriateness of the training: this should be consistent with the job and the related security responsibilities. How is it provided, internally or externally? If internal, is it a formal course or general 'on the job' type training? Who has provided the training, and are they suitably qualified? If the training is informal, is there some definition of what has been covered? If the training is external, who has approved the supplier? Is the supplier an accredited or industry-recognized provider of training? What records exist and do they reflect the nature and depth of training given?

As a minimum, organizations should have some form of induction training, which is given to all employees, contractors and third-party users. This should cover the general principles of security, the information security policy, areas of applicability, etc. This should be formally recorded in individual records. In addition, it should be ensured that sufficient training for those with more complex security responsibilities is in place, that all training material is up to date, and that the training is provided in time for the job to be carried out. Check the records for different types of job function, to ensure that sufficient training is provided, and that it is provided before access to information or services is given.

There will be situations, particularly with technical aspects, where experience or previously acquired qualifications are claimed in lieu of formal training. Auditors need to take a pragmatic approach on this and view the sum total of formal training, qualifications and experience when looking at the skills of individuals and how they fit with their roles. If previously acquired experience is claimed, make sure it is current and relevant: in what environment was it gained? Has it been verified in any way? Many organizations rely too heavily on what individuals claim in CVs – an inadequately trained or inexperienced individual in a key position can cause major damage to vital assets, so it is important that the organization treat this training issue seriously. This relates to the checks that should be made on recruitment (see 2.3.1.1).

The auditor should confirm that the organization provides appropriate training and keeps records of employee training activities. The auditor needs the organization to demonstrate that staff are '...aware of:...the information security policy;...their contribution to the effectiveness of the information security management system...; and...the implications of not conforming with the information security management system requirements' (ISO/IEC 27001:2013, 7.3).

2.3.2.3 Disciplinary process (ISO/IEC 27001:2013, A.7.2.3)

'There should be a formal and communicated disciplinary process in place to take action against employees who have committed an information security breach.'

Implementation guidance

Any non-compliance with the security policy or controls by employees needs to be properly dealt with or there will be a decline in standards and an increase in insecurity. The disciplinary process will be influenced by the organization's culture and personnel management practices but it should be documented and staff should be aware of the details. To avoid problems and demotivated employees, the disciplinary process should ensure fair treatment, and only start when there is evidence that a security breach or a non-compliance with controls, policies or procedures has taken place. There should be different grades of non-compliances considered in the disciplinary process, to be able to react accordingly to the grade and severity of the incident. Compliance incentives can act as an excellent foil to sanctions for non-compliance.

Auditing guidance

This might be a sensitive issue in organizations, but it is important that such a process is in place to be able to react properly to any security breaches, and to deter non-compliance. Auditors should check that employees are made aware of the disciplinary process, and that it provides fair treatment to all involved. If the disciplinary process is not implemented correctly, the organization might be liable to potential claims of unfair dismissal or other personal infringements. A disciplinary process should be defined, and without its deterrent, management effectiveness could well be compromised. Auditors should check with recorded security incidents, look at the criteria for disciplinary action and verify that such procedures are being effectively employed. Auditors should also check that procedures are in place to ensure that the disciplinary process is only used if there is sufficient evidence that a security breach or non-compliance has occurred.

2.3.3 Termination and change of employment (ISO/IEC 27001:2013, A.7.3)

Objective: To protect the organization's interests as part of the process of changing or terminating employment.

2.3.3.1 Termination or change of employment responsibilities (ISO/IEC 27001:2013, A.7.3.1)

'Information security responsibilities and duties that remain valid after termination or change of employment shall be defined, communicated to the employee or contractor and enforced.'

Implementation guidance

There are a lot of problems that can occur if termination or change of employment is not handled appropriately (see also 2.4.1.4 and 2.5.2.6). There should be processes in place ensuring that all rights for logical and physical access are removed as and when the job function terminates. Someone within the organization should be responsible for making this happen, ensuring that the necessary communications between departments take place in case of termination or change of employment. On termination, all equipment and information belonging to the organization or its customers should be returned as per company policy.

The responsibilities for termination or change of employment should also include ongoing security or legal requirements that might need to remain even after any business relationship has ended. The most typical example is the confidentiality agreement, and all such responsibilities and duties should be covered in the employee's, contractor's or third-party user's contract. Another important point that is sometimes overlooked is to apply all these controls not only in the case of employment termination, but also when an employee, contractor or third-party user changes jobs. A change of job should be handled as a termination of one job and the beginning of another, and all logical and physical access rights and all assets related to the old job need to be returned.

Auditing guidance

The auditor should confirm that the organization has procedures and responsibilities in place for the termination and change of employment. The auditor should look for records that provide evidence that these procedures and responsibilities are clearly assigned and executed, and that responsibilities have been appointed for the termination of logical and physical access rights and the return of assets (see also 2.4.2.3). There should be procedures in place to ensure that all parties involved in these actions are notified if a termination or change of employment takes place, as well as other parties who need to be aware of the event.

Another aspect for the auditor to consider is the handling of employee responsibilities or duties that continue for a period after the employment has terminated. The auditor should check records to identify whether such responsibilities have been included in the contract.

Finally, it should be confirmed that the responsibilities, controls and procedures applied in case of employment termination are also applied when the employment changes.

2.4 Asset management (ISO/IEC 27001:2013, Clause A.8)

2.4.1 Responsibility for assets (ISO/IEC 27001:2013, A.8.1)

Objective: To identify organizational assets and define appropriate protection responsibilities.

2.4.1.1 Inventory of assets (ISO/IEC 27001:2013, A.8.1.1)

'Assets associated with information and information processing facilities shall be identified and an inventory of these assets shall be drawn up and maintained.'

Implementation guidance

An asset inventory is a requirement of accounting standards, so for this reason, as well as for other information security reasons, all organizations should have such an inventory. Appropriate protection can only be properly applied to assets if it is known that the organization has them – only then can their information security, business and legal requirements be assessed.

For all assets, the inventory should contain information about their business value and classification (see also 2.4.2), and their backup and disaster recovery arrangements.

The inventory of physical assets should contain full details of equipment identity, including owner (see also 2.4.2.2), location, maker, model, generic type (e.g. printer, PC), serial number, date of acquisition and inventory tag.

A record of disposals – when and how/who to – also needs to be kept, and the asset inventory should be updated whenever an item is disposed of. Organizational inventory tags (logo, inventory number) should be fixed to all items that appear in the inventory. Information assets can be listed by application, perhaps as a list of database or file names. It should be ensured that all documentation (including system documentation), contracts, procedures and business recovery plans are included in the inventory; indicate the owner and those with operational responsibility.

All software products should also be listed in the asset inventory, where they are used and where the original media are kept, together with the relevant licensing information. Adequate procedures should be in place to maintain accuracy of the inventory and a stock check should be carried out at least annually.

Auditing guidance

The auditor should confirm that the organization maintains a complete and accurate asset inventory. This is to include all major information (in whatever form, including software), physical assets, services and processes to be protected. The assessment will first need to determine that assets have been properly identified and classified (see also 2.4.2). The auditor should evaluate the inventory's adequacy: is it complete and accurate? Does it contain all necessary detail, and when and how is it updated? Are disposals recorded, when and to whom?

The auditor should check that somebody has been given the responsibility for the asset inventory, for its development and maintenance. It should also be checked how the inventory is protected. If the inventory is computer based, what about access control and backup? If paper based, where is it kept, how is it protected against loss; and what happens when the record is replaced? Are old copies kept? If yes, for how long and where? The asset inventory should identify:

- the item, format and, where applicable, its unique serial number, date, etc.;
- its business value and security classification;
- owner;
- location;
- media (if information);
- licence (software);
- information about backups and disaster recovery;
- date of entry and/or audit check.

2.4.1.2 Ownership of assets (ISO/IEC 27001:2013, A.8.1.2)

'Assets maintained in the inventory shall be owned.'

Implementation guidance

Possibly the most important concept regarding responsibility for, and protection of, assets is to assign asset ownership. It is necessary to appoint an asset owner for all major assets, and this asset owner is responsible for the asset itself, and its protection. This includes:

- determining the classification of the asset (see 2.4.2.1);
- supporting risk assessments by giving input about the asset's business value and its importance for the organization's business activities;
- ensuring appropriate protection in the day-to-day use of the asset;
- keeping security classifications and control arrangements up to date.

It might be the case that the asset owner is not working with the asset on a day-to-day basis. In such cases, it is best that the asset owner appoints a custodian who works with the asset and looks after the asset on the asset owner's behalf. This custodian then looks after the protection of the asset in day-to-day business, but it is important to note that the owner remains ultimately responsible and needs to check that the custodian is taking the responsibilities seriously. As most organizations have a lot of assets and/or complex systems, it can help to consider several assets together, e.g. all assets involved in a particular business process or in the provision of a particular service. The owner of that process or service could then be responsible for all of the assets involved in the process or service, and for their correct functioning and provision.

Auditing guidance

The auditor should confirm that an owner has been assigned for all important assets, and that this owner is aware of the tasks and duties that come with asset ownership. It might be helpful to consider the records for asset classification and updates of this classification, to identify evidence that the asset owner is actually involved in these activities.

The auditor should also check the procedures in place to delegate routine tasks or the day-to-day use and protection of the asset to a custodian, and how, in case of such delegation, the owner checks that all tasks are carried out correctly.

As an asset inventory is only useful if it is up to date; the auditor should check the procedures in place to update the asset inventory, and how the introduction of new assets and the disposal of assets is reflected in the asset inventory.

2.4.1.3 Acceptable use of assets (ISO/IEC 27001:2013, A.8.1.3)

'Rules for the acceptable use of information and of assets associated with information and information processing facilities shall be identified, documented and implemented.'

Implementation guidance

Every organization is vulnerable to staff, and others, misusing assets, i.e. using them in any way that is different from the business purpose of these facilities. This might be unintentional or deliberate – in either case, there is a risk that misuse could imperil the integrity of data and systems, threaten availability and expose confidential information, or the information processing systems might be used to attack other organizations.

A typical example is the internet, which can be used for casual browsing during working time (which is possibly not the intended business use), or which can be used to launch an attack from the organization's network into other networks – an action for which the organization could be held liable.

In some circumstances, misuse of computers can be a criminal offence, e.g. in the UK under the Computer Misuse Act 1990. Similar legislation is in place in many other countries. The details of the applicable legislation should be checked, to inform control selection.

To ensure that assets are only used for their intended business purpose, the organization should identify, develop and implement rules, procedures and guidelines describing the acceptable use of the assets. These rules can vary considerably, depending on the asset considered. The intended business use, past incidents and the owner of the asset can give valuable input when developing the rules for acceptable use. Any different use should be considered as improper use, and all staff should be made aware of that.

It is important that everyone using the asset signs up to these rules, including not only the organization's employees, but also any contractors, third-party users or anyone else using the asset.

Auditing guidance

The auditor should confirm that acceptable use rules clearly describe the intended use of the assets, and also the limits of this intended use.

The organization should apply controls to be able to detect misuse that might take place. Disciplinary procedures should deal with actions on discovering intentional misuse (see also 2.3.2.3). Investigate the use of other, peripheral or associated equipment, such as printers and copiers: what is the policy here? Is a warning message displayed at log-on, making the user aware of the fact that unauthorized use of information processing facilities is not permitted?

The auditor should also confirm that users of the assets are aware of these rules – evidence should be that the rules have been signed prior to access to the asset being given. It might also be helpful to talk to users, and to look at incident reports, to identify where the rules of acceptable use have not been followed, or have not functioned as intended. If the organization has no rules for the acceptable use of assets in place, there should be valid reasons for not doing so, and these should link up with the findings of the risk assessment. Again, it might be helpful to look at incident reports, to identify areas where rules for acceptable use would be helpful.

2.4.1.4 Return of assets (ISO/IEC 27001:2013, A.8.1.4)

'All employees and external party users shall return all of the organizational assets in their possession upon termination of their employment, contract or agreement.'

Implementation guidance

The organization should have procedures in place to ensure that all assets in the possession of employees, contractors and third-party users are returned when their employment terminates or changes (see also 2.3.3). It is important that this covers all assets, not only equipment and software, but also all of the organization's documents and any information stored on media. Depending on the organization, its business and the particular job function, there might also be other assets, e.g. credit cards, access cards, manuals and mobile devices.

All of the organization's information that might have been stored on non-organizational assets, such as private equipment, or equipment of a third-party organization or of a contractor, should also be returned and securely erased from that equipment. The return of assets should be part of the contract.

Auditing guidance

Auditors should examine the procedures the organization has in place to ensure the return of assets. There are several issues that these procedures should address:

- they should cover all assets, ranging from hardware and equipment to information of any form (electronic, paper, on storage media, slides, films, etc.), and should also cover keys or cards that are used for access control purposes;
- they should also cover the transfer of any information stored or processed on non-organizational equipment or media, and the secure erasure of the information from that equipment or media;
- they should be applicable to employees, contractors and third-party users.

The auditor should also check that these procedures are applied not only upon termination, but also if the employment is changed and the assets are no longer required in the new job function.

2.4.2 Information classification (ISO/IEC 27001:2013, A.8.2)

Objective: To ensure that information receives an appropriate level of protection in accordance with its importance to the organization.

2.4.2.1 Classification of information (ISO/IEC 27001:2013, A.8.2.1)

'Information shall be classified in terms of legal requirements, value, criticality and sensitivity to unauthorised disclosure or modification.'

Implementation guidance

Information of different levels of sensitivity and criticality will require differing levels of protection and handling procedures that give this protection. A method of labelling called 'classification' should be used to identify the protection level for information. The classification scheme should be in writing and available to all those with authority to apply it – i.e. all those who originate documents and data. The classification scheme should also be easy to understand and clearly differentiate between the classification levels to support the correct assignment of classification levels.

Classified information requires a clear definition that will unambiguously indicate to staff when and how it should be used. Too many classes may lead to drift – staff forget the clear definitions and make a guess. Too few classification levels and staff will find that they may need to over- or under-classify.

There is no international standard for the classification of information. Most large organizations have a formal scheme and these can vary considerably. Similar labels are used (confidential, restricted, etc.) but their meaning, in terms of their value, criticality and sensitivity, can be very different – often because the organizations' business needs are different.

Procedures are required to specify the handling, storage and disposal requirements of each classification. Also, allowance should be made for the need to reduce the level of classification if the sensitivity reduces – and vice versa. Provide for change and expiry dates in these circumstances. The asset owner should be responsible for handling and updating the classification (see also 2.4.1.2).

Auditing guidance

Auditors should confirm that the organization has given due consideration to developing and implementing an adequate and consistent classification scheme, supported by guidelines. For assets to be properly protected, there should be some form of grading or classification giving due consideration to the key measures of confidentiality, integrity and availability. The classification should take account of business requirements for exchanging and sharing information, as well as the security requirements of the asset. The classification scheme should be applied to all assets considered in the scope of the ISMS. Without clear classification, assets may not be properly protected. The scheme should not be too complex and should be supported by arrangements with other organizations to ensure that the possible different classification schemes are understood: do the procedures account for how the correct classification is to be checked? Does a procedure to upgrade or downgrade the classification level exist?

The auditor should confirm that the classification scheme is readily accessible, understood by all staff and regularly reviewed. The owner of an asset should be responsible for its classification, and for updating the classification if anything changes.

2.4.2.2 Labelling of information (ISO/IEC 27001:2013, A.8.2.2)

'An appropriate set of procedures for information labelling shall be developed and implemented in accordance with the information classification scheme adopted by the organization.'

Implementation guidance

There is a risk of unauthorized disclosure, modification or destruction of classified material. All information items should be prominently labelled to ensure that they are given the necessary protection in use, storage and transport. All printed items should contain the appropriate classification label (unless unclassified) and unbound documents should carry it on every page.

Information held in information systems should also be classified, although it is sometimes difficult to label it. However, its classification should be maintained in the system or application documentation. This should be reflected in the system in terms of access levels and the range of users who can access it and at what level (read-only, write, delete). Some security systems include a security labelling facility. In any case, it should be ensured that the output (e.g. printouts) carry the label with them.

Transmitted information also requires classification. Low sensitivity information might be sent in an open email message but information of higher sensitivity may require encryption. The classification should be indicated in the text of the message. To maintain the security of information transferred within an organization or between organizations, appropriate controls need to be considered such as that defined in ISO/IEC 27002:2013, 13.1.

Care should be taken in interpreting classification labels on documents from other organizations because different organizations may have different definitions for the same (or similar sounding) label. Equally, ensure that your classifications will be properly respected when documents are sent to other organizations.

Information may cease to be sensitive after a certain period of time, e.g. when it has been made public. In such cases, provide an expiry date to avoid unnecessary protection expense.

Auditing guidance

The auditor should confirm that the organization has procedures for the labelling of classified information, compatible with the classification scheme. Auditors should also confirm that the marking correctly represents the most sensitive item in the entity (e.g. an information processing system or a database).

Labelling physical items, such as documents, tapes and hardware, is straightforward but what about information held in information systems, and correspondence electronically transferred? The auditor should confirm that the solution the organization has chosen for labelling electronic formats has been checked for adequacy: is this clear and understandable? Does it convey the correct label to the receiver of the information and does this subsequently lead to sufficiently secure access, use or storage of that information? Are the labels of physical assets appropriate? Labels may be hard to find, whereas they should be prominent; stick on labels can become detached and leave the item unmarked and unprotected.

2.4.2.3 Handling of assets (ISO/IEC 27001:2013, A.8.2.3)

'Procedures for handling assets shall be developed and implemented in accordance with the information classification scheme adopted by the organization.'

Implementation guidance

There is serious risk of a breach of confidentiality when sensitive information is being handled, e.g. invoices, cheques and financial transaction data. Additionally, breaches of integrity and availability also need consideration with regard to information assets. Procedures for the handling, processing, communication and storage of sensitive, critical or personally identifiable information, together with appropriate authorities and records, are required for the safe use of all these forms of information. Records should establish who is accountable for the information at all times, with clear handover from one person to another. Where carriers or couriers are transporting the items, ensure that there is a clear record of proven identity of the individual. All items should be clearly marked with the name of the ultimate recipient, who should provide a record of receipt.

Confidentiality or non-disclosure agreements need to be in place to protect information whilst it is being handled and processed as per ISO/IEC 27002:2013, 13.2.4.

Sensitive or critical items should be identified by risk assessment or, in the case of personally identifiable information, by a privacy impact assessment, and all activities and movements should be logged for later monitoring. The procedures should be adequate for the sensitivity level of the information being handled, in line with the classification applied (see 2.4.2.2). It is also important that these procedures cover all sensitive information, regardless of the form it takes.

Auditing guidance

The auditor should confirm that, for each classification label, there are procedures in place supporting information assigned that classification, such as procedures for secure processing, storage, transmission, declassification and destruction.

The auditor should confirm that procedures are in place to protect sensitive information – regardless of which form it takes – in line with the classification scheme used by the organization. Is it recorded? Who is responsible for this information? Who authorizes its release? Who has received the information, and who is authorized to access it? Is clear labelling applied? Is distribution of sensitive information only taking place if there is a need to know?

Where information is being handled by persons unknown to staff – such as couriers – what additional identity checks are made? Are access restrictions in place and, if so, which ones? Check that agreements with external parties support the classification and handling procedures that internal staff are required to follow, and that they provide appropriate interpretations for the classifications. Checks on confidentiality or non-disclosure agreements also need to be made (see 2.9.2.4).

Observe how people in the organization are handling sensitive, critical or personally identifiable information, and how easy or difficult it might be to circumvent or disregard the procedures.

2.4.3 Media handling (ISO/IEC 27001:2013, A.8.3)

Objective: To prevent unauthorized disclosure, modification, removal or destruction of information stored on media.

2.4.3.1 Management of removable media (ISO/IEC 27001:2013, A.8.3.1)

'Procedures shall be implemented for the management of removable media in accordance with the classification scheme adopted by the organization.'

Implementation guidance

Removable media containing the organization's data presents a serious vulnerability to loss of data and breaches of confidentiality. Controls are required in the management of media items, which could be tapes, disks, flash disks, removable hard drives, CDs, DVDs and printed media. Procedures should be developed and implemented to ensure that media are used, maintained and transported in a safe and controlled manner, based upon the classification of the information stored on the media. The supplier's recommendations on storage conditions should also be followed, and the issue of media deterioration should be considered.

Authorization should be required for the removal of any item from the premises for transport (see 2.4.2.3). The different authorization levels should be documented. Any risk assessment should recognize that the effectiveness of controls is limited by the ease with which small media items (e.g. USB sticks) can be removed from the premises.

Auditing guidance

The auditor should confirm that the organization has procedures for media handling in place, and that these procedures are followed and everybody is aware of them. The handling and storage should be appropriate for the classification of the information on the media, and the media should also be stored in accordance with manufacturer's recommendations.

Another aspect the auditor should check is how media are removed from the site: this might be for transfer to secure archive storage, by personnel for business use, or for destruction. There should be a well-defined procedure and logging mechanism in place, as well as authorization required in each case, as appropriate. The procedure should ensure that the removable media, if no longer needed, are erased to ensure that no information is leaked. If the media contain sensitive information, the auditor should check how they are labelled and handled, and confirm that there are procedures for the media to be destroyed or erased before being reused or discarded.

The auditor should also confirm that the transport arrangements for various media implement appropriate protection: does it have sufficient protection? Whatever controls are in place, this is a difficult area to police, so check that organizations have properly identified this in the risk assessment and whether any compensating controls have been applied.

2.4.3.2 Disposal of media (ISO/IEC 27001:2013, A.8.3.2)

'Media shall be disposed of securely when no longer required, using formal procedures.'

Implementation guidance

An item no longer required is often regarded as worthless. But if it contains information, it may well be of interest and value to others. Serious breaches of confidentiality occur when apparently worthless disks, tapes, paper files and printer ribbons are dumped without proper regard to their destruction. The return of damaged devices or media to the manufacturer for repair or disposal may also create a risk – the organization may not be able to retrieve data, but this does not mean that others cannot.

The procedures for the handling of classified information should cover the appropriate means of its destruction and disposal (see also 2.4.2.3), and there should be formal procedures in place governing the disposal of any media no longer required. Control 8.3.2 of ISO/IEC 27002:2013 describes what such procedures could address, and these controls should be applied as required by the importance and sensitivity of the information on the media. A record of sensitive items should be maintained at the point of destruction.

Auditing guidance

The problems related to removal of media from the site are covered above (see 2.4.3.1), but the auditor still needs to look at the disposal procedure issues listed in ISO/IEC 27002:2013, 8.3.2.

The auditor should confirm that formal procedures are in place: what general disposal arrangements are there? How do external contractors handle these? Check that the organization has carried out proper security and process checks and that the most sensitive level of information handled in this way is known and verified. It should be checked that – whatever the specific arrangements are – sensitive information cannot be compromised through the disposal process, because it has already been erased or destroyed. There should be a logging process of the disposed-of media, and what has been done to them prior to disposal; check that this provides a satisfactory audit trail.

There should also be a process to govern the handling of damaged media containing classified data, which should include a risk assessment and determine whether the media will be destroyed rather than sent for repair.

2.4.3.3 Physical media transfer (ISO/IEC 27001:2013, A.8.3.3)

'Media containing information shall be protected against unauthorized access, misuse or corruption during transportation.'

Implementation guidance

Transportation of media carries a risk of its loss, unauthorized access and misuse, with the related risk to confidentiality, integrity and availability of the information or software contained on the media. A risk assessment should be used to help select the right transport method and the controls applied to it (e.g. by post with recorded delivery, secure parcel delivery, personal delivery by trustworthy couriers). Appropriate courier services and packaging should be selected, including locked containers or tamper-evident packaging for sensitive or valuable items. It may even be appropriate to divide some consignments into two deliveries. To significantly mitigate the risk of breach of confidentiality if media are lost or stolen, consider encryption of data to be transported; if encrypting, never ship the encryption key and/or password with the encrypted data.

All despatches should be recorded and, where appropriate, authorized.

Auditing guidance

The auditor should confirm that whenever information is physically transported, the organization has considered what protection is in place to protect the media holding the information. What are the transport arrangements? If couriers, do they have secure and tamper-proof containers? Have they been identified as trustworthy couriers? Data might be transmitted by staff on disks or tapes, or perhaps on notebook computers – is this secure enough for the information carried? Who determines the method of transportation? What criteria do they use? Where couriers are employed, the methods of transportation might be the carrier's default methods: are these sufficient? Consider also postal services: are these secure?

The auditor should check for evidence of a risk assessment of sensitive or critical information, which should identify whether either encryption or other additional protections, such as digital signatures for critical information, are to be applied.

In all cases where there is a requirement for secure transportation of information, there should be formal procedures defining the arrangements, and the authority for release should be specified and recorded. Records should be kept of all deliveries, including details of what was delivered, when the courier picked it up, and when the delivery arrived at its destination.

2.5 Access control (ISO/IEC 27001:2013, Clause A.9)

2.5.1 Business requirements of access control (ISO/IEC 27001:2013, A.9.1)

Objective: To limit access to information and information processing facilities.

2.5.1.1 Access control policy (ISO/IEC 27001:2013, A.9.1.1)

'An access control policy shall be established, documented and reviewed based on business and information security requirements.'

Implementation guidance

Access control is the fundamental prerequisite to managing the user activities involving access to information or services on information processing systems. The confidentiality, integrity and availability of the organization's business information, services and processes, together with other business assets, are at risk.

Allocation of user access rights and rules should be driven by business requirements, decided by asset owners, and clearly stated in the access control policy. Any access not required by the business function(s) carried out should be forbidden. Failure to implement the access control policy effectively can very soon result in any form of unauthorized access, and this leads to the serious risk of unauthorized disclosure, unauthorized modification and loss of data integrity, and, ultimately, its unavailability while recovery takes place.

The organization should develop, document and implement an access control policy that defines user access rights based on business needs, taking into account the security requirements of the information, services, networks and/or applications accessed, and any legal or regulatory requirements. Standard user access profiles for specific jobs are a useful way of controlling access where many users are involved. It is important to review the access control policy regularly and remove any access rights that are no longer necessary. Note that business information repositories such as calendaring systems should also be taken into account.

Auditing guidance

Auditors should confirm that access control rights and rules are clearly defined in the access control policy document, and that the mechanisms for enforcement of this policy are in place and implemented. A given access right or rule should be traceable to a risk assessment and authorized by the asset owner. Any access to sensitive information or to information processing facilities should be based on the 'need to know' and 'need to use' principles. Any access granted should be based on the business requirements and be necessary for the job to be carried out. Role-based access should be implemented where possible.

Auditors should be prepared to question why certain roles, even senior ones, have access to certain information if the principle of 'need to know' appears not to be evident. Check also that access to sensitive information takes place in line with the classification given, and that the access rights given are not in conflict with applicable legislation or regulations. Also check that personnel with access to sensitive or confidential information have been properly trained, since unrestricted use of such information by untrained staff can have disastrous consequences.

The auditor should also check that the organization has procedures in place to review the access control policy, taking account of employees leaving the organization, job functions and requirements changing, etc. These procedures should include that any access rights that are found to be no longer necessary are removed immediately.

2.5.1.2 Access to networks and network services (ISO/IEC 27001:2013, A.9.1.2)

'Users shall only be provided with access to the network and network services that they have been specifically authorized to use.'

Implementation guidance

Major network services can provide a lot of individual services to thousands of users undertaking a wide variety of activities. Most users might only require two or three of these services. Each user should only have access to those services that they are actually authorized to use, in line with the access control policy (see also 2.5.1.1).

Additional control can be provided by restricting the use and views of the services. Where every user can see the full range of services, the organization can be vulnerable to unauthorized access attempts with the attendant risk of breach of confidentiality and loss of data integrity. Where restricting the use and views of services is not possible, alternative controls should be considered, such as preventing log-on from computers outside the organizational area to use a particular service. Particularly sensitive services might have to be implemented on a separate network domain or a separate system to be fully segregated.

Several network access controls, such as port level security, can be used to manage access to network services, and these controls should be implemented to support the organization's policy on the use of network services. Good change control and management is essential to keep the accesses correct, and regular monitoring is required to provide assurance.

Auditing guidance

Users logging on to a network, computer or application should have access only to the information and services required for their business function and that they have been authorized to use. What access is provided to which users needs to be explicitly defined and authorized. For some network services, total availability of the service and all information might not be a problem, for others it could be critical. The auditor needs to collect and check relevant evidence to be assured that the necessary access restrictions have been identified and implemented in a policy on the use of network services, in line with the access control policy (see also 2.5.1.1), and that the documentation reflects this. The auditor should also check that network security controls have been put in place to support the policy on the use of network services, and that the access controls have been incorporated into the design or configuration of the network.

2.5.2 User access management (ISO/IEC 27001:2013, A.9.2)

Objective: To ensure authorized user access and to prevent unauthorized access to systems and services.

2.5.2.1 User registration and de-registration (ISO/IEC 27001:2013, A.9.2.1)

'A formal user registration and de-registration process shall be implemented to enable assignment of access rights.'

Implementation guidance

Every user should be formally authorized and registered to each information system, network or service for which they have a business requirement to access. Failure to control registration can result in exposure of information to breach of confidentiality and the added risk of modification or loss.

The sharing of user IDs creates an especially risky vulnerability of a loss of accountability, which might also lead to problems with confidentiality, integrity and availability as the person doing something cannot be held accountable. All users should be accountable for all actions they are carrying out, and this is only possible with a unique user ID.

In those few cases where it is not possible to have individual IDs (e.g. because the system does not have the required functionality), consider applying a manual process to track who is using the ID, and to change the authentication credentials when the user of the ID changes.

Auditing guidance

The auditor needs to collect and check relevant evidence to be assured that the user registration and de-registration process functions effectively.

The term 'user' should be taken to include all users of information processing facilities, including system administrators, managers, application users, technical support personnel and programmers.

The process for creating and removing user IDs should be documented and logged. The process for employees leaving the organization should include prompt removal of user IDs. There should also be a process for auditing live IDs on a regular basis, to catch any that may have been inadvertently left live when they are no longer required. Redundant user IDs should not be reissued to other users because of the risk of inadvertently giving unauthorized access to resources.

The auditor should check to see if user IDs are unique or if they are shared. If shared, why is this necessary? Look at the management and authorization for this. Are additional controls applied to provide accountability, and are these additional controls sufficient?

2.5.2.2 User access provisioning (ISO/IEC 27001:2013, A.9.2.2)

'A formal user access provisioning process shall be implemented to assign or revoke access rights for all user types to all systems and services.'

Implementation guidance

The unjustified allocation of access rights increases the organization's vulnerability to breaches of confidentiality, loss of data integrity and unavailability through misuse.

A user registration form should be prepared, upon which the information system, network, service or application(s) required is described, as well as the conditions of access. This should be signed by the applicant as acceptance of the conditions and by the system owner as authority for the applicant to be registered. This form should have the user ID added to it and then be filed for the record.

It is equally important that user access to resources is promptly disabled on their ceasing to have a business reason to access the resources (e.g. termination of employment, internal job move), and procedures should be put in place to ensure this. There should be notification procedures and clearly defined responsibilities and actions if employees leave the organization, or change their employment.

Role-based access should be considered, as this can be easier to manage, and reduces the chances of 'special cases'; or, if they do appear, it makes them more visible and therefore harder to authorize without adequate justification.

Auditing guidance

The auditor needs to collect and check relevant evidence to be assured that access levels of all users are based on formal registration and authorization of the users, and that the access taking place is recorded. The auditor should check that these records are consistent with actual use: have staff who have moved away or changed to other responsibilities been immediately removed from this list? Interview staff who have changed role – do they retain old privileges?

Auditors should spend some time with the system administrators looking at operating system settings for access control of specific groups and individuals, ensuring that access can only take place for registered and authorized users. ISO/IEC 27002:2013, 9.2.1 gives further information on managing user IDs. It is also worthwhile checking that users are aware of their access rights and restrictions, and understand that they should not try to circumvent access controls.

2.5.2.3 Management of privileged access rights (ISO/IEC 27001:2013, A.9.2.3)

'The allocation and use of privileged access rights shall be restricted and controlled.'

Implementation guidance

Privileges are any features or facilities of information processing systems that enable the user to carry out system management activities or override access controls, such as maintaining the security system or the data management system. If privileges are uncontrolled, an increasing number of users will use privileges, rendering pointless the properly implemented access controls. The unnecessary allocation and use of privileges is often found to be a major contributing factor to the vulnerability of systems that have been breached. Loss of confidentiality through exposure, loss of integrity through modification of data and unavailability of data are typical consequences.

Privileged access to systems might be a difficult aspect for management to control. Systems engineers might try to persuade managers into providing a privilege that is not really required. Privilege is seen as an authorized means to shortcut well-placed controls. The fact is that most systems require very little use of privilege to manage them in a perfectly efficient manner.

Risk assessment should address not only the risk of providing privileges but also the consequences of not having them. Authorization should be provided at a senior level on the basis of a proper justification, which, in some cases, might need support from independent expertise.

An important need for special privilege can be in the event of a system failure. Fast recovery can require the skilled attention of a systems engineer who might need to access the internals of a system and to make changes that not only require privilege but also ignore controls that have been put in place to protect the system. Such occasions require their own controls, which will often be after the event. It is essential that all the actions that are taken are properly logged, assessed and reviewed, and that further checks of the system are made to ensure that its integrity has been re-established.

If strong identification and authentication techniques are required, the different techniques available (e.g. cryptographic means, smart cards, tokens or biometric means) should be considered and a risk assessment used to determine the best solution to meet the requirements of the organization.

What happens when the privileged person is not available? An emergency arrangement is required, such as a procedure to enable another systems engineer to obtain privilege out of hours. A user ID and password can be held in a safe under strict procedures for issue. This procedure should ensure that management will find out at the earliest convenient moment that the facility has been used, and should be followed up by review, as described above.

Auditing guidance

By definition, privileges provide access to system features that are normally limited. The audit should pay particular attention to system administrators, systems engineers and suppliers' engineers, and those whose job gives them 'super user' access to facilities. Auditors should check that – whilst this level of access should be restricted – at the same time more than one person should have the facility to have monitoring ability and the ability to supervise activities.

For critical functions, such as system administration, there should be a special user ID assigned solely for this purpose and logging of both the time and person initiating the event. Look for where these logs are required: how long are they kept? Can they be modified? When and under what circumstances are they reviewed? If the application does not provide this traceability, look again at additional controls to provide this.

Also check what happens in cases of incidents, such as system failures: are privileges allocated without due care and attention? Are controls violated? Check the records and logs that are created during such incidents. Also check that all privilege activities are monitored and logged, and that someone is responsible for reviewing these logs.

Access to secure information can include access to codes for safes and other secure areas: these also need to be recorded and regularly changed. It should also be verified that privileges are allocated on a 'need to use' and 'event-by-event' basis and are immediately removed when they are no longer necessary, and that a different user identity is provided from the one used for normal job functions.

It should be considered whether the authentication procedures used by the organization provide sufficient security for the information, systems and applications they are supposed to protect. The use of passwords alone is not generally appropriate for high-risk situations. A risk assessment should have been used to identify the appropriate user identification and authentication procedure.

2.5.2.4 Management of secret authentication information of users (ISO/IEC 27001:2013, A.9.2.4)

'The allocation of secret authentication information shall be controlled through a formal management process.'

Implementation guidance

User identification and authentication go hand in hand with access control, user registration and allocation of privileges. This is very often done through passwords, which are the main, but not only, mechanism for user authentication.

Whatever process is used for the allocation of secret authentication information, it should be based on the positive identification of the user and a formal process should be applied compelling users to change initial temporary passwords. The user should acknowledge the receipt.

A procedure is required to ensure that user IDs and passwords are issued only to those with a business need for access and are properly authorized by the owner of the resource being accessed. Where other methods of user authentication are being used, similar controls will be required but perhaps with additional controls relevant to the system being employed.

Auditing guidance

The auditor should check how secret authentication information is allocated and controlled; sometimes this is under the personal control of the user, but at other times the system administrator might issue it. If centrally controlled, where is the information held? Is this secure? Who has access? If it is under user control, are they aware of their responsibilities (see also 2.2.1.1)? Are procedures in place to ensure that temporary or default vendor passwords are changed immediately?

Auditors need to check that users have signed a statement to keep their secret authentication information confidential, and that they are aware of this responsibility. There should also be a record of how each user's identity was verified at the time of provision of the information, as well as a list of acceptable forms of ID. Look for records showing that initial secret authentication information has been changed by the user on first use. Ask users what happens when they forget their passwords: how are new passwords provided? Is there an 'unofficial' route for resetting passwords if the matter is deemed urgent?

2.5.2.5 Review of user access rights (ISO/IEC 27001:2013, A.9.2.5)

'Asset owners shall review users' access rights at regular intervals.'

Implementation guidance

Access rights should always be based on business needs – when the need has changed or has passed then the access should be cancelled. However, with the best will in the world, it is possible that a mistake may be made, and access inappropriately retained when a user leaves or changes role. The continued need for access should therefore be reviewed periodically and access rights should be withdrawn if it is found that they are no longer needed. This is particularly important where users have access to sensitive information or have special privileges to the system.

Auditing guidance

Auditors should check that procedures for the regular review of all kinds of user access rights and privileges are in place and followed. This might be a formal audit to check compliance, followed by a management-level review to check for consistency with business and policy requirements. Changes should be reviewed as a matter of course on a periodic basis.

Access control procedures should include reviews of the allocated access rights, they should be logged, and an authorized person should acknowledge that the users listed continue to have authority for the access rights.

2.5.2.6 Removal or adjustment of access rights (ISO/IEC 27001:2013, A.9.2.6)

'The access rights of all employees and external party users to information and information processing facilities shall be removed upon termination of their employment, contract or agreement, or adjusted upon change.'

Implementation guidance

If an employment situation terminates (i.e. for an employee, contractor or third-party user), all access rights associated with the employment should be considered for removal. This includes physical access rights (i.e. returning of access control cards, keys, identification cards, etc.; see also 2.4.3.2), as well as rights to log into the organization's network and user accounts, and use passwords and email addresses, as well as any other form of permitted access. Unless there are clearly identified reasons why particular access arrangements need to remain, all of these access rights should be removed immediately. It might also be necessary to update the documentation listing the people who have access rights, subscriptions that are tied to the person leaving or memberships in interest groups.

The same actions should take place when the employment changes. This might seem to be 'over the top', as the relationship with the organization is maintained, but it is appropriate. The main principle of all access controls should be to allow only access necessary for the job function, and any other access that is not explicitly allowed should be forbidden. Therefore, all forms of access should be reconsidered when employment changes and any access that is not necessary for the new job role should be removed.

Special procedures might be required if an employment termination is initiated by management and/or relates to disgruntled employees, contractors or third-party users, to avoid information collection and disclosure, or modification or destruction of information or services in the last minutes of employment.

Auditing guidance

The auditor should check that the organization has procedures in place that define all actions to be taken to remove access rights in case of employment termination. These procedures should be applied in case of any termination, irrespective of whether this relates to an employee, contractor, third-party user or anyone else having had access to the organization's premises or assets. The access rights to be considered for removal should include all physical and logical access, access to services and involvement in user or interest groups. The procedures should cover the notification of staff and other relevant parties of the departure of the user, with instructions to cease to share information with the user to which the user should no longer have access.

It is important that these procedures are also applied in case of employment changes, and the auditor should look for evidence that access rights are always removed if there is no defined business purpose for having them. The auditor should also check that employment termination or change initiates a review of all related user access rights (see also 2.5.2.5), and that all shared passwords the person had access to are changed.

2.5.3 User responsibilities (ISO/IEC 27001:2013, A.9.3)

Objective: To make users accountable for safeguarding their authentication information.

2.5.3.1 Use of secret authentication information (ISO/IEC 27001:2013, A.9.3.1)

'Users shall be required to follow the organization's practices in the use of secret authentication information.'

Implementation guidance

Exposed (written down) sensitive authentication information, or obvious and easily guessed passwords, can lead to misuse of systems by unauthorized persons, with the attendant risk of breaches of confidentiality, loss of integrity and unavailability of data. ISO/IEC 27002:2013, 9.3.1 contains guidelines for users for choosing their passwords, and for managing all forms of secret authentication data.

Users should also be made aware of the fact that they might be held accountable for actions carried out by someone else having used their sensitive authentication information.

Auditing guidance

The auditor should check that the policy on sensitive authentication information changes and password frequency, length and content is sufficient for the security requirements of the organization and the information being protected. Some systems enforce rules of this type, others do not: check what other measures are in place if the system does not automatically enforce such rules. If necessary, ask staff to show you how they change their sensitive authentication information (as relevant): do they know the criteria? Are the codes currently used consistent with policy?

The auditor should also check for instances of sensitive authentication information that are written down on memos, stuck to monitors, etc., or ask for the results of password-cracking tools that the organization might have used to check the quality of user passwords. ISO/IEC 27002:2013, 9.3.1 gives examples of good practices that should be followed. Check also the relation to other sensitive authentication information management controls, such as 9.2.3 and 9.4.3, and ensure that all these controls together build a good sensitive authentication information management system. Auditors should ensure that proper management authority is obtained when investigating use of sensitive authentication information.

2.5.4 System and application access control (ISO/IEC 27001:2013, A.9.4)

Objective: To prevent unauthorized access to systems and applications.

2.5.4.1 Information access restriction (ISO/IEC 27001:2013, A.9.4.1)

'Access to information and application system functions shall be restricted in accordance with the access control policy.'

Implementation guidance

The business owner of an application and the information held in the application should develop access rights and rules for this application, in accordance with the business requirements and the access control policy (see 2.5.1.1). These should define who will have access and, in the case of information, at what level, e.g. read, write, delete. Without these there is a high probability that users will be given access to too much information. This creates the risk of a breach of confidentiality and a loss of integrity or availability. Over-accessibility can also lead to the possibility of fraud in financial applications.

Be particularly cautious where a shared database is used. Ensure that each group of users can only access the data meeting the group's requirements, and that applications cannot be used to circumvent the access controls in place.

Auditing guidance

Auditors should collect and check relevant evidence to be assured that access to information provided by individual applications matches the business requirements and takes place in line with the access control policy (see also 2.5.1.1). For example, different applications might access the same database: can sensitive information be accessed from one program but not from another?

In many cases, users should not be aware of information or application functions that they are not allowed to access, so menu options that are not accessible for security reasons should be removed, likewise information in user manuals relating to sensitive functionality. Pay particular attention to little used parts of applications, such as maintenance utilities: are these properly controlled?

Auditors also need to check what happens to information that is accessible: do users have read and write permissions, and is this necessary? Are there restrictions to its output? It should be ensured that information is protected in line with the classification scheme.

2.5.4.2 Secure log-on procedures (ISO/IEC 27001:2013, A.9.4.2)

'Where required by the access control policy, access to systems and applications shall be controlled by a secure log-on procedure.'

Implementation guidance

While a log-on process should be user-friendly, it should not disclose any information about the operating system, service or application the user is trying to access. Any information provided might be helpful for an unauthorized person trying to get access – the least information given away the better.

Some systems do not have the facility to control or modify this aspect and the user has no choice but to accept the system as provided; in such cases, other supporting controls should be used. Users should implement what features are available and introduce compensating controls where necessary.

ISO/IEC 27002:2013, 9.4.2 provides more details of what a secure log-on procedure should provide, and as many aspects as possible of that list should be implemented in the organization's operating systems.

Auditing guidance

Log-on procedures can be more involved than simply typing the correct name and password. The auditor needs to collect and check relevant evidence to check the implementation of the log-on procedures. Does the user need to go through a series of log-on activities? What happens if the wrong information is entered? Is there a delay period, and is a lockout situation imposed after repeated false attempts? If so, what is the recovery mechanism? Is the password displayed or hidden? Is it obvious how many characters the password should have?

ISO/IEC 27002:2013, 9.4.2 provides a list of properties a secure log-on procedure should have. Sometimes an application might not provide the necessary level of log-on protection, e.g. if the number of unsuccessful log-ons is not restricted. In this situation, determine if any other controls have been added, e.g. by physically restricting access to the operating system. The risk assessment should have considered each operating system and application, the access methods and log-on procedures, and whether these are considered adequate – check for this.

2.5.4.3 Password management system (ISO/IEC 27001:2013, A.9.4.3)

'Password management systems shall be interactive and should ensure quality passwords.'

Implementation guidance

Weak password management leads to vulnerability to misuse of systems by unauthorized persons, with the attendant risk of breaches of confidentiality, loss of integrity and unavailability of information. Where systems provide automatic controls over password quality and frequency of change, these should be used. If this is not the case, compensating controls and monitoring might be required.

ISO/IEC 27002:2013 contains guidelines for good password management systems in control 9.4.3, and also further guidance about password management and the related user responsibilities in controls 9.2.4 and 9.3.1.

Auditing guidance

The auditor should check that there is a policy covering the use of passwords throughout the organization, including ensuring that a secure password management system is used. Any additional requirements for particularly sensitive areas should be additional to, and consistent with, this policy, where possible. Aspects that auditors should check for include:

- length and make-up of passwords;
- frequency of changing passwords;
- use of individual user IDs;
- use of common passwords between individuals and access applications;
- secure handling and storage of passwords;
- changing of default passwords.

Additional desirable attributes of a password management system are included in ISO/IEC 27002:2013, 9.4.3. Look also at the process for the changing of passwords: what logs are kept? Are old passwords disallowed? Does the application require verification before accepting a new password – e.g. double entry? If necessary, get users to demonstrate how passwords are changed.

2.5.4.4 Use of privileged utility programs (ISO/IEC 27001:2013, A.9.4.4)

'The use of utility programs that might be capable of overriding system and application controls shall be restricted and tightly controlled.'

Implementation guidance

System utilities provide an opportunity for misuse, which can damage the integrity of the security controls of an operating system or application. As these utilities are nevertheless needed when control problems arise, their use should be tightly controlled and only take place after sufficient authorization.

It is essential that all system utilities are identified, that the associated risks are assessed and that controls such as those described in ISO/IEC 27002:2013, 9.4.4 are applied.

Auditing guidance

System utilities might allow access to parts of the system that applications do not, and might also allow overriding of system controls. Auditors should collect and check relevant evidence to establish that the organization has overall control on the utilities installed: check that they are known and authorized for use, and that appropriate access control and use restrictions are applied. Check on individual systems that no additional or modified utilities are installed.

In less well-regulated environments, unauthorized utilities might have been installed that could have consequences not only for the confidentiality of information but also for its integrity and availability. The auditor should check that no forgotten utilities are still resident on systems that should have been removed. Finally, the auditor should check that no one without appropriate authorization can access or use system utilities. Further controls to secure the use of system utilities are provided in ISO/IEC 27002:2013, 9.4.4.

2.5.4.5 Access control to program source code (ISO/IEC 27001:2013, A.9.4.5)

'Access to program source code shall be restricted.'

Implementation guidance

Program source code contains details on the operational system and implemented controls. It provides a perfect starting point for unauthorized modification of a system. Serious security problems can result from unauthorized access to, and modification of, program source code.

Strong procedures are required to ensure proper maintenance and protection of the program source code. One method is to use central storage of such code, e.g. in a library. Such libraries should not be held in, and should not be accessible from, operational systems, and there should be access controls and procedures in place to manage the libraries and the program source code. Other controls include logging of copies sent, after authorization, to maintenance staff and the subsequent updates, the application of strict change control procedures, and the usage of digital signatures to enable unauthorized modifications to be identified.

Auditing guidance

The auditor needs to check that access to any program source code is protected, ideally by not holding it on operational systems and by strictly controlling the access to it. Access to such code and the means to modify, recompile and re-link it can effectively bypass all of the security features normally imposed by the application. Highly secure applications might need some means of verifying object code checksums (or digital signatures) to be used to identify whether changes have been made.

The auditor should also check any macros and database report programs; these can be much easier to change and could cause loss of integrity, or make information unavailable. Normal update and reintroduction of application source code also needs to be properly controlled to prevent installation of the wrong code, and to ensure recording and testing of changes before access to live data is permitted. Auditors should look for documented procedures and records relating to these activities.

ISO/IEC 27002:2013, 9.4.5 provides additional guidelines that should be applied to secure access to program source code and the libraries in which this code might be held. The auditor should also ask about other standards that have been used for securing code.

2.6 Cryptography (ISO/IEC 27001:2013, Clause A.10)

2.6.1 Cryptographic controls (ISO/IEC 27001:2013, A.10.1)

Objective: To ensure proper and effective use of cryptography to protect the confidentiality, authenticity and/or integrity of information.

2.6.1.1 Policy on the use of cryptographic controls (ISO/IEC 27001:2013, A.10.1.1)

'A policy on the use of cryptographic controls for protection of information shall be developed and implemented.'

Implementation guidance

The effective use of cryptographic techniques is only possible if some basic principles are identified, agreed and applied. For example, the algorithms used should be suitable for the business processes and services they are supporting, the key length should be appropriate for the security requirements of the information that will be protected, and the solutions implemented should be consistent throughout the part of the organization where cryptographic controls are applied.

In order to achieve this, a risk assessment should be used to determine the requirements for confidentiality, integrity, authenticity and non-repudiation, and the most suitable cryptographic solutions and a policy on the use of cryptographic controls should be communicated to all users of such controls prior to any application. This policy should take into account the relevant key management activities (see also 2.5.1.2) and legal issues involved in the use of cryptographic techniques.

For example, the organization might want to retain copies of the employees' encryption keys to avoid any misuse, such as the unauthorized distribution of the organization's information or a disgruntled employee first encrypting information and then destroying the encryption key.

Auditing guidance

An important aspect of the secure and effective use of cryptographic controls is to make sure that the requirements have been identified and that the right decisions have been made about what cryptographic controls to use, and to have a policy in place supporting the day-to-day use of these controls. This policy should cover the key management approach applied (see ISO/IEC 27002:2013, 10.1.2 and below), the roles and responsibilities related to the use of cryptographic controls, and the information and circumstances for which cryptographic controls should be applied.

If the organization applies cryptographic controls, auditors should check that a policy on the use of cryptographic controls has been developed and communicated, and is known and followed by employees. The auditor should question whether the decisions that have been made are supported by the results of a risk assessment, and whether the controls used are commensurate with this policy.

The strength of cryptographic controls does vary and is related to the algorithms employed and the key sizes and parameters used. A factor to be taken into account is the environment and application in which cryptographic controls are to be applied. Some application environments might require the use of stronger cryptographic controls.

Therefore, auditors will need to have at least a general knowledge of cryptographic techniques and mechanisms, and key management, and their application to assess whether what the organization is using is adequate or appropriate. The use of specialist technical expertise may also be necessary to support the auditor during the audit.

2.6.1.2 Key management (ISO/IEC 27001:2013, A.10.1.2)

'A policy on the use, protection and lifetime of cryptographic keys shall be developed and implemented through their whole lifecycle.'

Implementation guidance

The key management system used should provide protection of the cryptographic keys according to their use, and according to the management methods that support the handling and use of keys as required by the business processes for which the cryptographic controls will be used.

The requirements for key management will be different depending on which cryptographic technique, and secret or public key technique, will be used and what type of key, public or private, is considered. The protection of secret and private cryptographic keys is different from the protection necessary for the public keys. When defining a key management system, these protection requirements should be analysed with the help of a risk assessment and appropriate protection should be in place before the first keys are generated and used.

A set of standards and procedures for the key management activities as described in ISO/IEC 27002:2013, 10.1.2 should be agreed and implemented before using cryptographic controls. The lifetime of cryptographic keys should be defined for each application in relation to the risks of possible damage if they are compromised and the deactivation of keys should take place immediately when this time period is finished.

The organization should also consider its needs for keeping copies of keys or parts of keys used for cryptographic controls, either for its own use or to satisfy legal requirements. It might be necessary to agree with certification authorities details about the management of public keys, and the organization might also want to consider the use of other services, like key generation, distribution and revocation, directory services or time stamping, offered by third-party organizations.

Auditing guidance

Key management is an essential prerequisite for the secure use of cryptographic controls, and no cryptography should be used without a secure key management system in place. The whole life cycle should be considered (see ISO/IEC 27002:2013, 10.1.2 for a list of events that comprise the life of a key).

Auditors should check that the organization has implemented adequate controls to protect:

- secret and private keys against replacement, disclosure, modification and destruction;
- public keys and public-key certificates against replacement, unauthorized modification and destruction; if the organization is using a certification authority (public or internal) for the management of its public keys, it should be ensured that this certification authority is adequately protected, trustworthy and suitably managed.

The protection of cryptographic keys should encompass both logical and physical protection. Auditors should review the physical and logical access controls that are being applied to protect cryptographic keys. Where keys are managed by, or in combination with, third parties, the organization should have agreements in place that cover keys' protection.

In addition, auditors should check that the other key management procedures, as described in ISO/IEC 27002:2013, 10.1.2, are in place. If a key escrow or key recovery mechanism or process is applied to cryptographic keys, it should be ensured that the appropriate employees are aware of it, and that there are no possibilities to circumvent key escrow, or to substitute an unauthorized key.

2.7 Physical and environmental security (ISO/IEC 27001:2013, Clause A.11)

2.7.1 Secure areas (ISO/IEC 27001:2013, A.11.1)

Objective: To prevent unauthorized physical access, damage and interference to the organization's information and information processing facilities.

2.7.1.1 Physical security perimeter (ISO/IEC 27001:2013, A.11.1.1)

'Security perimeters shall be defined and used to protect areas that contain either sensitive or critical information and information processing facilities.'

Implementation guidance

Premises that contain business processes, information, services, IT and other assets are vulnerable to unauthorized access and undesirable activities of people. Some of those people might also work for the organization, so internal protection is required as well as external.

Small premises might be a single domain with just one obvious perimeter. Larger premises might need to use several perimeters to be divided into several domains. It is important to define the perimeter of each domain properly.

The objective is to be able to control entry into (and possible exit from) every domain, and additionally to record entry to, and exit from, sensitive areas. A security model can be prepared showing, perhaps schematically, the various domains and the access points between them. A risk assessment should be used to define appropriate perimeters and to select controls to give adequate protection. Procedures should be provided regarding the management of physical security, and access control and its monitoring. Give due consideration to out-of-hours working and any necessary authorization, supervision and monitoring. The implementation guidance of ISO/IEC 27002:2013, 11.1.1 contains a list of guidelines and controls for physical security perimeters.

Auditing guidance

All organizations should be able to demonstrate to auditors the physical protection of their assets. Where major installations are involved, security procedures should describe what measures are taken, how these are monitored and who has access. To assess the physical protection in place, auditors will need to look for potential breaches: open fire escapes, unattended reception areas, sharing of security passes and unlocked cabinets are all potential security threats and should be noted. A part of the physical protection in place is the use of physical perimeters, so the organization should be able to explain what perimeters are in place, and what protection is achieved with them (this should be supported by a risk assessment). Auditors should also check how the access into the building is controlled and monitored, and whether the controls in place are sufficient for the needs of the organization, or whether there are possibilities to circumvent the protection. The implementation guidance of ISO/IEC 27002:2013, 11.1.1 describes several different issues that should be considered and implemented for the security perimeters in an organization.

2.7.1.2 Physical entry controls (ISO/IEC 27001:2013, A.11.1.2)

'Secure areas shall be protected by appropriate entry controls to ensure that only authorized personnel are allowed access.'

Implementation guidance

A secure area in this context is any area that the organization identifies as requiring access control, ensuring that only authorized personnel have access. Such areas might include the entire premises but certainly computer rooms, telecommunications rooms and closets, and plant rooms (power, air conditioning). A clerical area handling sensitive data, such as telesales, customer service or banking, might also fall into this category. Different areas will possibly need different levels of security and access control. Secure areas and the protection provided by the controls within such areas should be determined by a risk assessment.

The threats include breaches of confidentiality and unauthorized tampering with, or theft of, equipment (loss of integrity or availability).

Appropriate entry controls might extend from a check of organization ID cards to an electronic check of personal identity, including the entry of a password or personal identification number (PIN). It should be ensured that all people accessing secure areas are appropriately checked and that badges are used to identify authorized people. It should also be ensured that visitors are registered and escorted, and that any person not wearing an identification badge is reported to security personnel. Further specific controls are listed in the implementation guidance of ISO/IEC 27002:2013, 11.1.2.

Auditing guidance

Auditors should check the entry controls in place and ensure that these are sufficient to restrict physical access to authorized people only. Do employees wear badges and is this mandatory? What about visitors? Are badges issued? Is their entry and exit logged? What restrictions are placed on their movements? Are persons not wearing badges challenged? Auditors, invariably being visitors to the organization, can determine this from their own treatment.

Auditors should also check the audit trails of the access that has taken place in the past, and ensure that procedures for the review and update of the physical access rights are in place. Authorization in terms of access rights and restrictions might be in a variety of forms: they could be described in job descriptions, they could be written into procedures or they could be listed at the point where the restrictions apply, such as a label affixed to a door, for example. Auditors should take a view on the appropriateness of each approach.

2.7.1.3 Securing offices, rooms and facilities (ISO/IEC 27001:2013, A.11.1.3)

'Physical security for offices, rooms and facilities shall be designed and applied.'

Implementation guidance

The organization should identify the controls required to secure offices, rooms and facilities; these controls should be suitable for the value and importance of the assets within the areas. In addition, care should be taken that all applicable health and safety regulations and standards are complied with.

It is important to avoid giving clues about the information processed in buildings, e.g. using signs pointing to the server room or indicating the purpose of rooms or buildings. For the same reason, directories and internal phone books should not be accessible by anyone outside the organization.

The risk of loss of confidentiality, integrity and availability all increase as more of the organization's key information is moved to one place. These premises become increasingly critical to the organization. Especially effective security is then required, both outside and inside, to ensure that losses are not experienced.

Auditing guidance

The level of protection provided for a secure area should be consistent with the most sensitive and critical information held in this area, in line with the procedures for the handling of classified information. There is a clear link here to risk assessment; auditors should confirm that the information security requirements have been identified and that the protection in place is adequate for this.

A list of security controls that might be applicable to protect secure areas is given in the implementation guidance of ISO/IEC 27002:2013, 11.1.3. Auditors can also confirm compliance with health and safety regulations and standards, and can try to identify the use and purpose of rooms where information is processed, or try to get access to internal telephone directories, to test these controls.

2.7.1.4 Protecting against external and environmental threats (ISO/IEC 27001:2013, A.11.1.4)

'Physical protection against natural disasters, malicious attack or accidents shall be designed and applied.'

Implementation guidance

The organization might be affected by problems outside its control. The selection and design of the site and the controls applied should take account of the possibility of damage from fire, flooding, explosions, civil unrest and other forms of natural or man-made disaster. Consideration should also be given to any threats presented by neighbouring accommodation.

The selection of controls should be carried out in consultation with specialists in the relevant areas, documented as required in ISO/IEC 27001, 6.1.3, and the necessary training recorded in staff training records. The fallback arrangements and backups taken should conform to the business continuity plan (see also 2.13.1).

Auditing guidance

Auditors should check the provisions the organization has in place to react to natural and man-made disasters, and the physical protection in place to limit the damage. Records should exist of specialist advice pertaining to the main hazards that are likely in the circumstances, and should identify measures that are to be taken.

Have any sources of hazard been omitted? For example, if a neighbouring site poses a threat to the organization, has this been considered? The auditor should also investigate whether these arrangements link in with, and conform to, the business continuity arrangements the organization has implemented (see also 2.13.1). Another issue to consider is the emergency support and environmental protection in place. Has the organization assessed whether there is a fire hazard or whether the site could be flooded – and what is there to prevent or mitigate these dangers?

Auditors should check if the measures have been implemented as described. It might be helpful to walk through the site to identify weaknesses, such as large quantities of paper stored on an aisle without specific protection, not easily accessible fire extinguishers or a computer room in the basement. Some measures may be eroded by time (e.g. fire extinguishers being used to prop fire doors open on hot days).

2.7.1.5 Working in secure areas (ISO/IEC 27001:2013, A.11.1.5)

'Procedures for working in secure areas shall be designed and applied.'

Implementation guidance

In addition to setting up physical perimeters, applying entry controls and securing offices, rooms and facilities for day-to-day operations, the specific security requirements of areas involving sensitive work need to be considered. For example, an organization could be working on a new product, the design of which has high commercial value and is ahead of its competitors. Another example might involve similar circumstances where an organization has a project or process that is sensitive and needs to be protected from damage, loss, modification or disclosure.

Therefore, the work in secure areas should be protected and supervised as described in the implementation guidance of ISO/IEC 27002:2013, 11.1.5. Which controls exactly are applied and the degree of protection achieved with them should be determined by a risk assessment, based on the work going on in the secure areas, and the protection requirements of the assets in these areas.

Auditing guidance

Personnel working in secure areas should be subject to specific controls that ensure sufficient security is implemented for the sensitive and critical information that is processed in such areas. Auditors should check:

- the entry controls in place to ensure that only authorized personnel have access to secure areas;
- to what extent the work going on in such areas is generally known and whether this exceeds any rules on 'need to know';
- how easy or difficult it is to take information (e.g. in the form of paper or disks) in or out of such areas;
- whether it is possible to take photographic, video, audio or any other recording equipment inside such areas and to use or leave such equipment there to record;
- whether the work in such areas is sufficiently supervised and whether mechanisms are in place to ensure that dual controls are applied (where the presence and simultaneous activity of two individuals to authorize an action are needed), where appropriate.

The auditor should also check that the procedures for working in secure areas are applied consistently to employees, contractors and third-party users.

2.7.1.6 Delivery and loading areas (ISO/IEC 27001:2013, A.11.1.6)

'Access points such as delivery and loading areas and other points where unauthorized persons could enter the premises shall be controlled and, if possible, isolated from information processing facilities to avoid unauthorized access.'

Implementation guidance

Breaches of confidentiality, integrity and availability can occur through uncontrolled public access to the organization's premises, and uncontrolled delivery and despatch. There are threats from unauthorized access, malicious delivery (e.g. a letter bomb) and unauthorized despatch, which frequently involves theft.

A busy organization will experience a lot of deliveries and collections. No one will be surprised to see packages being delivered or collected by strangers (delivery staff). It is therefore essential to control this activity to ensure that deliveries are expected and collections are of only properly authorized despatches, and that delivery staff are properly controlled with respect to access. In addition, the delivery and loading area might be easily accessible by the public, and as there are people coming and going, someone might use the chance to sneak into the organization's premises.

In order to control these problems, a segregated area is recommended, which isolates delivery and loading from the most secure areas and restricts access from outside to identified and authorized personnel. Internal procedures should be used to ensure that the transfer of goods between loading bay and secure area is controlled, and that the incoming goods are inspected for potential threats. Complete records of all deliveries and despatches should be kept, and the incoming and outgoing material should be reflected in updates of the asset inventory (see also 2.4.1.1). The names of all delivery drivers and vehicle numbers should be recorded.

Auditing guidance

This control is to help prevent security incidents by public access, and delivery and loading operations. Deliveries may involve outside personnel on the premises and their movements need to be restricted, as well as the public access that might take place via the delivery and loading area. Products received could cause a hazard if not properly inspected, tested or stored as appropriate. Items leaving the premises could inadvertently contain sensitive information.

The auditor should check that the risks relevant to loading and delivery areas have been identified by the risk assessment and security procedures have been implemented and adequate measures taken to both prevent and mitigate the potential security breaches. For example, how are goods received: by the person requiring the goods, a stores employee, or a general receptionist? What happens to the goods after receipt: are they sent directly into the secure area? Are they held in a store? Are they left on someone's desk? Are they included in the asset inventory (see also 2.4.1.1) upon receipt, and is the asset inventory also updated when goods leave the organization? How is the access to the delivery and loading area controlled? Is it possible for the public to gain access, and what controls are in place between the delivery and loading area, and other parts of the organization? Do staff know what to look for (e.g. evidence of tampering), and how to react?

2.7.2 Equipment (ISO/IEC 27001:2013, A.11.2)

Objective: To prevent loss, damage, theft or compromise of assets and interruption to the organization's operations.

2.7.2.1 Equipment siting and protection (ISO/IEC 27001:2013, A.11.2.1)

'Equipment shall be sited and protected to reduce the risks from environmental threats and hazards, and opportunities for unauthorized access.'

Implementation guidance

Equipment at the location of work can be vulnerable to damage and interference with a resultant loss of integrity and availability. Accessibility can lead to unauthorized use and breach of confidentiality of the information displayed.

Physical damage can arise from poor environmental conditions, particularly in industrial situations where moisture, dust and chemicals can all take their toll. Electrical and electromagnetic interference can be significant in some environments and should be tested to identify possible problems resulting from interference. It is relatively easy to protect equipment such as communications devices and connection panels – simply lock them in an appropriate small room or equipment cupboard. Equipment required by operating staff should be available in their workspace and special protection, such as keyboard membranes, can help to protect it. Ensure that the risk assessment covers this kind of situation and identifies solutions for equipment requiring special protection.

Other problems relate to the people working with the equipment – equipment can be damaged if eating, drinking or smoking takes place too close to the equipment; there should be a policy in place to prevent this. In addition, there are risks associated with equipment displaying confidential information. There are different ways to handle this, including a clear desk and clear screen policy (see also 2.7.2.9), rules for unattended equipment (see also 2.7.2.8) and the restriction of the viewing angle to avoid information being viewed by unauthorized people, e.g. when walking past.

Where networked equipment is considered, remember that remote equipment probably requires more security attention than in-house equipment. Clearly establish the bounds of the organization's network responsibilities and apply appropriate protection at the boundaries. Ensure that remote equipment is accounted for in inventories, security scope and risk assessments.

A list of guidelines is provided in ISO/IEC 27002:2013, 11.2.1.

Auditing guidance

During the audit, organizations need to demonstrate how their equipment is protected from environmental threats and hazards, and opportunities for unauthorized access. Equipment should be sited away from potential risk areas, such as windows that could be easily broken during a burglary without setting off an alarm. Consider also that terminal screens might be viewed from outside the protected area and information leaked through electromagnetic or other emanation (e.g. the sound of keystrokes).

In some environments it may be appropriate to secure computer equipment to desks. As well as malicious damage, equipment needs to be protected from accidental damage from a very untidy or poorly managed environment, unrestricted access, unstable racks, spilt coffee, etc., and from environmental hazards, such as water, chemicals and fire, and electromagnetic interference. Check that such measures have been considered, a risk assessment has taken place, and that adequate protection is implemented.

Looking beyond the immediate computer area, does a fire or water hazard exist in adjacent areas? A large organization will probably have a site layout plan; look for this, and see how it was developed.

2.7.2.2 Supporting utilities (ISO/IEC 27001:2013, A.11.2.2)

'Equipment shall be protected from power failures and other disruptions caused by failures in supporting utilities.'

Implementation guidance

Supporting utilities, such as electricity supply, water supply, heating/ventilation and air conditioning are an essential prerequisite to ensure business continuity and for the use of any computing and communications equipment. While we tend to take a reliable public supply of electricity or water for granted, we are still at risk of disruption resulting from incidents, such as the activities of someone with a digger – no supporting utilities, no availability.

The need for supporting utilities should be identified; the utilities should be regularly inspected and tested, to ensure their reliable functioning. The water supply should be sufficient to guarantee air conditioning, as necessary, as well as sufficient fire protection. A problem with any of the essential supporting utilities should be identified by an alarm system.

The risk assessment should highlight those facilities that require redundant power supplies, especially for computer services supporting critical business operations. The selected option, such as an uninterruptible power supply (UPS) or generator, should be capable of sustaining sufficient power for the maximum potential period of power cut, or at least for the time identified in the business continuity plans. Some equipment requires a very 'clean' electrical power supply, free of peaks and troughs (spikes) in power. If this requirement is not met, power spikes can lead to a loss of availability through equipment damage or failure.

Auditing guidance

The necessary level of protection provided from disturbances in supporting utilities depends on the security requirements and the criticality of the equipment and the information held on the system. For example, high availability requirements should result in the choice of suitable controls to ensure sufficient supporting utilities. Auditors should check that the organization has considered all necessary supporting utilities and has implemented controls to ensure adequate provision. They should also check that there are procedures in place to inspect and test all supporting utilities regularly, e.g. by looking at the records of these tests.

For higher power requirements, check that sufficient facilities, such as standby generators, UPS units and redundant array of independent (or inexpensive) disks (RAID) units, are in place. If this is the case, look closer at the power supply support: does it have sufficient capacity to cover air conditioning requirements? What is the extended operating period; does it match the documented requirements? How is this verified? Is equipment maintained and tested in accordance with the manufacturer's recommendations? What actions are taken to detect malfunctions? The auditor should also check that emergency lighting is provided in case of a power failure.

The auditor should also check that there are redundant connections to utility providers, to prevent failure of one connection resulting in a loss of service.

2.7.2.3 Cabling security (ISO/IEC 27001:2013, A.11.2.3)

'Power and telecommunications cabling carrying data or supporting information services shall be protected from interception, interference or damage.'

Implementation guidance

Unless properly installed, it can be very easy to damage such cables, especially their connectors, leading to a loss of availability; it can sometimes be difficult to trace the fault. Cables left on floors and hanging loose around walls are a safety hazard and will suffer excessive wear, or pulling, leading to damage. In addition, unclearly marked cables might be subject to inaccurate connection. Finally, including power and data cables in the same conduit may result in interference in the data cables.

In sensitive businesses, communications cables might be at risk of interception and consequent loss of confidentiality of the information they carry, in which case they should be protected by conduits, with all connections made in locked equipment rooms or boxes. While physical protection will be the principal safeguard to consider, there are also data transmission controls, such as encryption, that can be employed. The risk assessment should determine where this is necessary.

Public access to roadside telecommunications junction boxes might also pose a risk in some places, both from physical damage and from tampering. Discuss this with your network service provider with a view, perhaps, to relocating the box underground beneath a secure lid. The implementation guidance in ISO/IEC 27002:2013, 11.2.3 provides further guidance on cabling security, especially on how to protect sensitive or critical systems.

Auditing guidance

During the audit, the organization should be able to demonstrate that interconnecting plugs and cables are adequately protected from interception, interference or damage: are they correctly fitted and properly routed, or are they badly put together and placed where they could be damaged or cause an accident? ISO/IEC 27002:2013, 11.2.3 provides a list of guidelines that should be considered for power and telecommunication cables.

A good indication of the status of the cables is the documentation describing the power and communication lines, and the cable markings used. Routing of communications links could be critical for some users. Auditors should check that the organization has considered the communication risks and looked for potential weak points regarding network cabling, such as cabling routed between departments or buildings, unprotected or unsegregated telecommunication and power lines, or cabling accessible to interruption or eavesdropping.

2.7.2.4 Equipment maintenance (ISO/IEC 27001:2013, A.11.2.4)

'Equipment shall be correctly maintained to ensure its continued availability and integrity.'

Implementation guidance

The correct operation of computing and communication equipment can lead to a false sense of security. The sudden failure of equipment that has worked faultlessly for years can have a profound effect on the integrity and availability of business processes and services – especially if the equipment cannot readily be replaced.

Most equipment is supplied with maintenance instructions and these need to be built into operating procedures. Ensure that maintainers are authorized and qualified, and that they are accompanied when carrying out their maintenance work. Keep records of faults and maintenance – monitoring these will help in the judgement of when equipment should be replaced and so avoid the sudden failure. Also ensure (either by deleting confidential information prior to maintenance activities or protecting it in other ways) that no confidential information is disclosed.

Auditing guidance

Auditors should confirm that the organization has controls in place to ensure equipment maintenance in accordance with suppliers' recommended service intervals and specifications. In addition, simple operations such as regular cleaning of air filters, tape drive mechanisms and printers can save considerable disruption. Even mundane activities such as regular disk defragmenting on computers can extend the usable lifespan of equipment.

Look at what maintenance activities are identified in the procedures, determine whether they are sufficient and check the records to ensure that maintenance activities in the past have taken place as specified in the procedures. There needs to be a formal fault reporting mechanism; check for this and for logs of defects and their rectification. It should be verified that only authorized personnel can carry out maintenance activities, that external personnel carrying out maintenance are accompanied at all times, and that no confidential information is accessed. As far as is possible, equipment should be checked after repairs and maintenance for evidence of tampering and unauthorized modification (e.g. the installation of a wireless access point to permit future remote access).

2.7.2.5 Removal of assets (ISO/IEC 27001:2013, A.11.2.5)

'Equipment, information or software shall not be taken off-site without prior authorization.'

Implementation guidance

Assets removed without authorization might be in the process of being stolen. This can lead to non-availability, and loss of confidentiality where items contain information or software. In a technology-rich environment, the risk of loss can be very high, especially among items that can be useful at home. Also consider the possibility of the unauthorized removal of information via the internet for later retrieval at home.

Equipment, information and software, etc. should not be taken (or transmitted) off-site without formal authorization. It is essential that the organization should know where its assets are and who has control over them. All items of equipment should, where possible, be marked to indicate their ownership.

Those carrying items, such as laptops, mobile devices and sensitive business information (in digital form or on paper), in and out on a regular basis should be provided with documentation verifying their authority to carry this equipment with them, which should be produced on demand.

Where items are on long-term loan, for instance, to home workers, the individual should be required to endorse the inventory periodically to the effect that the items are still in their possession, in good condition and necessary for their work. Procedures should be implemented to ensure that those leaving employment return all company assets before departure.

Those bringing property in should be required to log the property on entry so that they can leave with it without difficulty. Appropriate documentation should be kept regarding procedures, authorizations, off-site inventory and returns.

Auditing guidance

In many organizations, staff can regularly be expected to take equipment, data and documents away from the premises. This might be to work at home, or to attend meetings at other premises. For some organizations, controlling this might cause a problem. The auditor should confirm the organization has identified both the problem and how to effectively control it. There are three main alternatives that might be considered, as follows.

1. Removal of assets containing sensitive information is prohibited. On the face of it, this is the simplest approach but difficult to implement for the majority of organizations. Highly restricted environments might need to use this approach.

2. Removal of assets containing sensitive information is permitted under appropriate controls. The organization needs to be very clear what information is involved and what controls are needed.
3. Removal of assets containing sensitive information is permitted without control. This can be very dangerous and should not be chosen if not accompanied with additional controls regulating the handling of sensitive information outside the organization's premises.

The auditor should check which approach is taken and then look at the documented procedures for control. Is a booking in/out system in use? What authorization is needed and recorded? Is this for all items or only a restricted range? How does management monitor compliance? Are spot checks carried out? Does the confidentiality agreement (see 2.9.2.4 and ISO/IEC 27002:2013, 13.2.4) cover responsibility for information held while off-premises? Many employees use notebook computers: what controls exist for these or any sensitive data held? Information held on notebook computers or storage media could be disguised by changing the file names: are search tools needed to combat this? If so, when are they employed?

Ease of communications now means that information removal off-site no longer has to use physical media. Auditors should also check what transfer control mechanisms exist when accessing, for example, the internet.

2.7.2.6 Security of equipment and assets off-premises (ISO/IEC 27001:2013, A.11.2.6)

'Security shall be applied to off-site assets taking into account the different risks of working outside the organization's premises.'

Implementation guidance

The security of equipment off-site should be subject to a risk assessment and appropriate controls should be used to ensure that it remains in place and in operation, and does not provide an uncontrolled risk, e.g. through its links to central networks. The risk assessment should ensure that the security provided off-site is equivalent to the security arrangements on-site, and the appropriate insurance arrangements should be considered for equipment off-site.

Be especially careful to identify all the risks inherent in portable equipment. Portable/mobile devices are particularly vulnerable to theft when in public places, leading to breaches of confidentiality as well as the loss of the device. The security of mobile equipment is also discussed in 2.2.2.1.

Auditing guidance

Use of equipment outside the secure environment of the organization yields many security problems and added threats. Therefore, the auditor should check that the controls implemented for the physical protection of equipment outside premises give adequate security, comparable with what is achieved on-site. Procedures and guidelines should be in place to ensure that equipment off-premises is not left unattended, and that, where relevant, sufficient insurance is taken out.

For some organizations, this will not be an issue, depending on the business carried out, but for most organizations this could be a significant area of concern. The auditor should look for evidence that the risks posed by equipment off-premises have been assessed, where this is applicable to the organization. Additional protection mechanisms are also described in 2.2.2, where 2.2.2.1 addresses mobile computing, and 2.2.2.2 the security issues related to home workers and their environment.

2.7.2.7 Secure disposal or re-use of equipment (ISO/IEC 27001:2013, A.11.2.7)

'All items of equipment containing storage media shall be verified to ensure that any sensitive data and licensed software has been removed or securely overwritten prior to disposal or re-use.'

Implementation guidance

Serious breaches of confidentiality can occur when discarded storage media, such as disk drives, are accessed by unauthorized persons, e.g. after being sold on the second-hand market. Although files may have been deleted from media, they may remain accessible to anyone with the right tools. Copies can also be made of the organization's software if it is not permanently deleted, laying the organization open to charges of unauthorized distribution of copyright material. The organization should use controls to ensure that any equipment to be disposed of, or re-used, no longer contains sensitive information. It should be noted that certain storage devices (such as magnetic hard drives) may be adequately wiped by the use of suitable programs, but that other types of devices (such as solid state disks) may retain data indefinitely. Many types of storage device are relatively cheap; the organization should consider complete destruction as a method of disposal for unwanted storage devices containing sensitive data.

Encrypted data may not be retrievable from discarded media in any reasonable time if the keys are suitably chosen and not stored on or with the media, but, as computing power increases, the risk of successful brute force decryption also rises.

Auditing guidance

The auditor should check that the organization has an effective process in place to ensure that any sensitive information is removed from equipment that is disposed of or otherwise taken outside of its control. The auditor should also check user awareness of the potential dangers. The organization should also understand that erasing files from magnetic media is not secure: the information is often still accessible. Overwriting tools should be utilized to reduce the chance of this.

For very sensitive systems, specialist equipment might be needed to remove residual magnetic data from disks and tapes. The policy might need to extend to all media – the labels of items holding sensitive data could be removed before disposal making positive identification difficult.

Depending on the risks involved, physical destruction of media could be the best option, and this should also extend to hard disks inside computers. Some organizations might consider this a drastic step but magnetic storage is relatively cheap – much cheaper than the loss or compromising of sensitive data. Consider also items sent for repair: are there any checks to ensure that sensitive information cannot be accessed or interfered with? Also see 2.4.3.2.

2.7.2.8 Unattended user equipment (ISO/IEC 27001:2013, A.11.2.8)

'Users shall ensure that unattended equipment has appropriate protection.'

Implementation guidance

An unattended system, logged on to a service, is vulnerable to misuse, providing concerns for confidentiality, integrity and availability. Other equipment that is accessible by unauthorized people is also vulnerable to disclosure, misuse, tampering and theft, leading to loss of confidentiality, integrity and/or availability.

Sensitive equipment, such as communications panels and controllers, should be locked away in equipment rooms or purpose-built cupboards. Desktop equipment such as computers should be locked or shut down when unattended. Risk assessment should determine the maximum time a session can be left open before it is automatically disabled or terminated. Keyboard and mouse use should be protected by a password while the computer is unattended. Screen savers with passwords should be used to hide the screen contents while unattended. Ensure that the strength of the password system is sufficient for the resources being protected.

Auditing guidance

Auditors should check that the appropriate procedures to secure all unattended equipment are in place, checking that staff are aware of the requirements and dangers, and ensuring that the procedures are followed. Look for instances of unattended terminals without password protection or left logged on. Screen savers on PCs should have some password protection – check. Ask to turn on any terminals switched off and ensure access to information is not possible.

Timeouts from specific sessions should be considered where any public access or access by less security-cleared personnel is possible. Look at where this has been defined, and determine whether the periods allocated are sufficient given the access level, the vulnerability and the operational needs. Determine what the timeout is based on: specific use of the application or simply movements of a mouse cursor. Check that this timeout is employed consistently at all locations under high risk – particular public offices might have a number of sessions requiring this protection, so check that they all work. Where timeouts rely on an operating system feature such as a screen saver, check that the facility is not disabled and, of course, check that password use is according to policy.

High-security equipment such as network servers and communications equipment, normally left unattended, should be in some protected environment – check for this and whether it is properly secured.

2.7.2.9 Clear desk and clear screen policy (ISO/IEC 27001:2013, A.11.2.9)

'A clear desk policy for papers and removable storage media and a clear screen policy for information processing facilities shall be adopted.'

Implementation guidance

Offices, especially open-plan offices, provide good opportunities for people to walk around and read documents or information on screens that they are not authorized to view. Such people might be other staff or outsiders, e.g. visitors, cleaners. The availability of technology means that it is a simple and quick operation to steal a paper or copy it, returning the original without being noticed. Since most people have a camera in their pocket (as part of their mobile phone), photographing documents on paper or on a screen is also very easy and unobtrusive. If access to computers is not protected, this might lead to unauthorized persons obtaining sensitive information. Confidentiality is easily compromised, information might be modified, and theft leads to non-availability.

A disorderly desk may lead to the loss of documents due to misfiling, or even putting them in the wastepaper bin by mistake, which could cause sensitive information to be viewed by unauthorized persons (such as recycling contractors). Information left out on desks is also more likely to be damaged or destroyed in a disaster such as a fire, flood or explosion.

Printers and fax machines may also pose a risk, and the use of pull printing (where the user has to authenticate to the printer before their job is printed) may be appropriate, as long as users know not to wander off while a particularly long document is being printed. Fax machines expected to receive sensitive data should be suitably located, and regularly checked for messages.

Organizations should adopt a clear desk policy for papers and computer media, and a clear screen policy for information processing facilities, in order to reduce these risks. Staff usually see this as an onerous control, so training should emphasize the benefits of working in an organized and tidy environment, and mandate that screen savers with passwords are used, or equipment is switched off when leaving the office. Compliance should be monitored, persistent offenders noted and sanctions applied.

Auditing guidance

The objective of this control is to ensure both that sensitive information in any form (processed electronically, on paper or media, etc.) is not left unattended, and that information is not lost or made available to unauthorized people. This should apply to both working and non-working hours. Controls applied should be suitable for the given classification of information (see also 2.4.2).

The auditor should confirm that the organization has a policy in place to prevent sensitive information being accessed by outside staff, e.g. cleaning staff. The auditor should also check what happens when desks, filing cabinets and safes are left unattended during the day. Furthermore, the auditor should check what happens when cleaning staff or other visitors (such as the auditor) enter the office. Furthermore, is there a process for warning staff who may be working on sensitive data, so that they can clear their screens and/or desks before the visitor enters? The auditor should check the risk of access to computers while staff are absent (irrespective of the duration of this absence): password-protected screen savers, switching the computer off, or any other form of clear screen control should be applied.

Are fax machines and printers suitably located? Is there a pile of printouts on the printer and/or fax machine?

Where necessary, additional access controls should also be in place. If the whole area is covered by an appropriate level of security, and all staff are appropriately authorized, then additional measures might not be needed. Check that the overall policy is clear, and that staff are aware of, and follow, the appropriate procedures. Sanctions for non-compliance should be simple and consistently applied.

2.8 Operations security (ISO/IEC 27001:2013, Clause A.12)

2.8.1 Operational procedures and responsibilities (ISO/IEC 27001:2013, A.12.1)

Objective: To ensure correct and secure operations of information processing facilities.

2.8.1.1 Documented operating procedures (ISO/IEC 27001:2013, A.12.1.1)

'Operating procedures shall be documented and made available to all users who need them.'

Implementation guidance

As with all the controls in this standard, the scale of implementation should be appropriate for the size and complexity of the particular organization. A large organization with many staff involved might require more comprehensive and detailed procedures than a small organization, where a few thoroughly experienced staff cover the whole operation. The documentation requirements for these procedures might also vary. In any case, the organization should ensure that sufficient documentation is available to address typical activities in the day-to-day working environment, e.g. computer start-up and close-down procedures, backup, equipment maintenance, media handling, computer room and mail-handling management, and safety. Typical instructions that operating procedures should specify are described in ISO/IEC 27002:2013, 12.1.1.

Inadequate or incorrectly documented procedures can result in system or application failures, causing loss of availability, failure of data integrity and breaches of confidentiality. Complicated or infrequently used procedures provide opportunities for mistakes and require particular care in their drafting. Operating procedures should be treated as formal documents, changes to which may only be approved by authorized persons.

Many organizations outsource the operation and management of their computers and communications to a specialist facilities management organization. One way of ensuring that appropriate security is in place is to use sufficiently detailed contracts and to check whether the other organization is ISO/IEC 27001:2013-compliant (see 2.11.2 for more about working with service providers).

Auditing guidance

Auditors should check the organization's operating procedures and confirm that these are appropriately documented and are being applied throughout the relevant parts of the organization. In order to be able to check procedures for completeness, auditors should have a general understanding of the various operational processes and workings of the organization.

In addition, the handling and management of these procedures should be checked. A check should be made to ensure that it is not possible to modify the procedures without appropriate authorization, that proper version control is in place, and that the latest version is accessible to all those who need to have access to it.

Another aspect to check is the level of compliance with these procedures: is it possible to circumvent these procedures or any associated controls? Are employees aware of these procedures, and do they know which procedure to use and where to find it, if needed? Are they using the latest version?

Responsibility for network service operation and administration is often held by a separate department or even a separate organization. The auditor therefore needs to understand the arrangement in place and confirm that the necessary levels of service and procedures are properly documented. In some areas, detailed work instructions will be needed. There is likely to be considerable use made of supplier documentation, so this should also be checked for relevance and availability. This issue is also addressed in more detail in 2.11.2.

2.8.1.2 Change management (ISO/IEC 27001:2013, A.12.1.2)

'Changes to the organization, business processes, information processing facilities and systems that affect information security shall be controlled.'

Implementation guidance

Uncontrolled changes to the organization, its processes, information processing facilities and systems can cause major interruptions to business processes. Changes that might cause problems include the installation of new software, changes to a business process or operational environment, acquisition of a new business or the introduction of new connections between information processing facilities and systems.

In order to avoid interruption to business activities, any changes to operational systems should only take place after the necessary testing has taken place and formal approval has been given. The procedures for such an approval should take into account the potential impacts, including on security controls in place.

The change procedure should also allow for fallback arrangements and for aborting changes, if necessary, and define what action is needed to recover from unsuccessful changes. All changes that are made need to be fully documented, e.g. in an audit log that contains all relevant information.

Care should also be taken to control the changes to applications (see also 2.10.2.2) since these changes are likely to have an impact on the operational systems in which these applications are running.

Auditing guidance

The auditor should check that management responsibility and formal procedures are in place to control changes to operational information processing facilities. All such changes should be monitored and logs should exist describing exactly which changes have been made. It should be confirmed that no changes can take place without first assessing the possible information security impact such changes may have, and obtaining appropriate approval for the proposed change.

The auditor should check that procedures are in place describing how to react if something goes wrong, and it should be confirmed that no change can take place without appropriate fallback procedures allowing a return to the original state. Auditors should confirm that the procedures also cover informing all relevant personnel when a change has taken place. A good indication can be obtained by looking not only at the change control procedures, but also at records of previous changes, to check that these records contain all necessary information and support the evidence that the change control procedures have been complied with. If operational changes also yield changes to the applications, the changes should be integrated (see also 2.10.2.2).

2.8.1.3 Capacity management (ISO/IEC 27001:2013, A.12.1.3)

'The use of resources shall be monitored, tuned and projections made of future capacity requirements to ensure the required system performance.'

Implementation guidance

With growing requirements for the use of information processing facilities, an organization may be vulnerable to loss of service due to inadequate resources, both facilities and staff. This risk should be reduced by system tuning and monitoring the use of present resources and, with the support of user planning input, projecting future requirements. Controls detecting problems in capacity can ensure timely corrective action. This is especially important for communications networks where changes in load can be very sudden, resulting in poor performance and unproductive users.

Capacity should also be managed by managing demand wherever possible, to smooth out peaks and troughs. Alternatively, if using externally provided services, it may be possible to arrange for on-the-fly increases and decreases in capacity to match demand.

The capacity management process is likely to be cyclical and evidence of requirements should be obtained and documented in a standard manner that enables reliable repeat capacity calculations to be made. Critical systems, such as network gateways and main database servers, should be prioritized, and a capacity management plan documented for them.

Auditing guidance

Forward planning of basic operational needs is often overlooked and auditors should check the organization's ability to handle this. The first question could be: 'What is being monitored?'. This would typically include disk capacity, transmission throughput, printer utilization and other potential bottlenecks. Other appropriate questions could be: 'What do you use for system tuning?'; 'Where are the logs from the detection controls put in place to identify capacity problems?'; and 'How do you manage demand?'. Examples of methods for managing demand are given in ISO/IEC 27002:2013, 12.1.3.

The auditor should enquire how the information received from the capacity monitoring is used to identify future capacity requirements. Trending information and extrapolation of future requirements should be being used to plan upgrades. This should include capacity figures, trended as appropriate, reviews, and identification of needs and upgrade plans. Look also at staff planning: inadequate human resources at critical times can often compromise security.

2.8.1.4 Separation of development, testing and operational environments (ISO/IEC 27001:2013, A.12.1.4)

'Development, testing, and operational environments shall be separated to reduce the risks of unauthorized access or changes to the operational environment.'

Implementation guidance

Operational systems demand the utmost integrity and reliability. Using the same equipment and software to develop and test new systems makes the organization's operational systems vulnerable to failures of integrity and loss of availability. Risks are particularly high where new operational software, communications equipment or services are being developed or tested. Errors and omissions can lead to unauthorized access, introduction of malicious code and plenty of other security problems.

Equally, it is highly inappropriate to put sensitive data into a test environment unless this is as secure as the live environment, taking into account the fact that, since you are testing something, it may have security flaws. Hence any security controls that are part of the application or other entity being tested should not be considered part of the effective control set for the test environment.

Measures such as strong access control should be applied to separate development, testing and operational environments. The easiest way is to use entirely separate systems, or at least separate domains that are completely segregated from each other. Wherever such a separation cannot be completely achieved, separate log-on procedures, supporting access control and good monitoring, can be implemented to achieve similar effects. Finalized and fully tested developments should be fed into the change control procedure in readiness for operational acceptance (see also 2.8.1.2 and 2.10.2.2).

Auditing guidance

It is important that separation between testing, development and live environments is achieved to avoid disruptions in the operational process. Therefore, the auditor should check how such separation is implemented, and what authorization processes ensure that development and untested application software are not used on operational systems. The auditor should also check in the risk assessment that this problem has been given appropriate consideration, and that the controls in place are adequate to protect against the identified risks.

If operational applications software and information are held on the same system as those under development and testing, then the auditor should check that they are at least held in separate domains, and that strong access controls are in place to ensure that no mixing of development, testing and operational environments takes place.

Different log-ins with different passwords should be necessary for operation and development. Test systems and compliers, system utilities, facilities to edit programmes, etc. should not be accessible from operational systems. The auditor should check how new software is introduced (see also 2.8.1.2), and that this software is no longer in the development or testing state.

If sensitive data is present in the testing environment, the security measures there should be at least as good as those in the live environment, neglecting any measures that are part of the system/software being tested; thus, additional security controls may be needed for the testing environment to take account of this.

2.8.2 Protection from malware (ISO/IEC 27001:2013, A.12.2)

Objective: To ensure that information and information processing facilities are protected against malware.

2.8.2.1 Controls against malware (ISO/IEC 27001:2013, A.12.2.1)

'Detection, prevention and recovery controls to protect against malware shall be implemented, combined with appropriate user awareness.'

Implementation guidance

Most (if not all) operating systems are vulnerable to the threat of malware (e.g. viruses, worms, Trojans). It is very easy for malware to install itself on a vulnerable system, but it can be difficult and costly to get rid of it. Prevention can only be achieved to a certain level (relatively new viruses, for example, are often not detected by the antivirus software), but it is still necessary that this control is strictly applied and followed. Malicious code in a networked system can have a devastating impact on the confidentiality, integrity and availability of all files on it, and potentially on any data that its users have a right to access. Traditionally, malware has affected only executable programs. However, macro viruses in word processing and spreadsheet files are a cause of significant difficulty because such files are quite commonly passed from user to user, and other forms of malicious code can spread to any file in the system.

One of the keys to prevention is user awareness. If staff understand the risks, they will apply the controls and will be wary about what to download, what emails to open and which websites to visit. It is advisable to use controls that run independently in the background, carrying out all necessary checks automatically. A separate check for malware using a different antivirus program should also be implemented where appropriate, such as on network file servers supporting a large number of workstations.

Another key to success is to ensure that the protection against malware is up to date. It is recommended that dynamic updates be used to ensure that the protection remains effective, and that key information sources are reviewed for news about the latest threats. Updates should be done manually if dynamic updates are not possible for technical reasons.

Auditing guidance

Malware is a problem on almost all operating systems; therefore the auditor should confirm that implemented controls are adequate. The guidance in ISO/IEC 27002:2013, 12.2.1 should be applied to ensure optimum protection.

A number of options are available when installing software protecting against malicious code. Sometimes it is held on a central server covering all client systems that are logged on. Other systems require the protection software to be installed on each system. Sometimes the installation updates the entire software package, and at other times libraries only are involved, so auditors need to know how to determine correct versions. Another important item for the auditor to check is that the updating is done whenever it is necessary, e.g. through an automatic update or some other form of notification of necessary updates. Handling of portable systems can involve particular problems: how are regular updates assured? Is malware protection available, or necessary, for the device in question?

For systems handling sensitive information, the use of more than one vendor's antivirus software is advisable, to improve detection rates.

If checks are not constantly running in the background (very often a good option, but not always possible), procedures should be explicit about regular checking; there should be a clear policy on incoming software, emails and websites. The auditor should also check the user awareness regarding this issue, and look at training records to ensure that users are aware of the correct behaviour.

The actions in the event of virus infection should be covered; check that automatic removal is implemented where possible. Occurrences of malicious code infections should be properly recorded. Look at the type of software used: is it adequate and properly supported?

Free packages from, for example, the internet, might not give the necessary protection and could cause additional damage; some malware imitates protection software in order to extort money from the user. The auditor should confirm whether users know and use the correct methods of interfacing with applications, operating systems, etc. An unexpected request for password information, for example, could be an attempt by an attacker to obtain a password and access vital data.

2.8.3 Backup (ISO/IEC 27001:2013, A.12.3)

Objective: To protect against loss of data.

2.8.3.1 Information backup (ISO/IEC 27001:2013, A.12.3.1)

'Backup copies of information, software and system images shall be taken and tested regularly in accordance with an agreed backup policy.'

Implementation guidance

Every organization is vulnerable to the crashed disk or failed tape and to a lot of other problems that can cause loss or corruption of information or software. Integrity and availability of all important information and software should be maintained by making regular copies to other media. The regularity will depend on the criticality of the data. Some systems can justify real-time backup – writing the copy at the same time as the original. If this is not possible, other copying should be used, be it automated or user initiated. A backup cycle should be designed to ensure that all information and software is copied at appropriate intervals while maintaining at least two copies of each file. This can, for instance, be satisfied with a three-tape cycle. Risk assessment should be used to identify the most critical data, which may justify more frequent copying.

Copies should be stored in a safe place. Full copies of data should be kept off-site or at least in a fireproof safe, and the protection applied to the backups should be as sound as that used for the original. It is important to regularly test the ability to restore data from backup.

Some data should be kept in a long-term archive. It is essential to maintain the means to recover data that has been archived. This requires the appropriate computer, media reading device and software to read the data format, e.g. database manager, and the correct version of the application programs to interpret the data fields. Failure to recover data could leave the organization in breach of statutory requirements to maintain records. Comprehensive records of tape contents and program/data relationships should be maintained.

Auditing guidance

Backups are a key component in maintaining information and software integrity and availability. The organization should have well-defined procedures for dealing with backup. Initially, look at the backup sequence, which needs to be consistent with the business and the security requirements, and compatible with recovery and business continuity plans.

In a typical network environment, this is based on full server backup plus a number of incremental updates defined at a frequency appropriate for the requirements for integrity and availability, e.g. daily, weekly or monthly cycles. The auditor should confirm that there are appropriate backup arrangements in place according to the results of the risk assessment, and check that these include full coverage of items within the ISMS scope.

How and where the backup media are labelled and stored is also important: the auditor should check that each item can be positively identified, is logged correctly and is held securely. Backup media should be held in separate locations to the systems they backup, and sufficient controls should be in place to give the same level of protection the backed-up information normally has.

The auditor should confirm what the long-term storage requirements of critical data are: how does the organization validate this? Backup media can deteriorate and need to be refreshed. Also look in the backup procedures for: what corrective actions are required if the backup fails?

What arrangements exist for restoring the data? How often is this exercised? What records are kept? Are backup media tested to ensure they are working properly? Test restoring of backup files should not compromise data integrity: check that this is adequately addressed. The auditor should check that requirements for business continuity planning (see also 2.13) are met by the backup arrangements in place in terms of frequency, media and availability.

2.8.4 Logging and monitoring (ISO/IEC 27001:2013, A.12.4)

Objective: To record events and generate evidence.

2.8.4.1 Event logging (ISO/IEC 27001:2013, A.12.4.1)

'Event logs recording user activities, exceptions, faults and information security events shall be produced, kept and regularly reviewed.'

Implementation guidance

Audit trails are an essential prerequisite to investigating what went wrong. They are often necessary to establish the events leading up to an incident as well as to determine the indisputable accountability for an incident.

The policy for event logging should be determined by an appropriate level of management. Some systems can produce very large logs covering a wide range of activities, exceptions and events within the system. Generally, such a mass of data is difficult to use to identify possible misuse. The level, type and frequency of monitoring will depend on the sensitivities of the system and should be established from the risk assessment. It is as important as the creation of monitoring logs to assign responsibilities and sufficient time to review these logs; information important for system processing might require more frequent reviews than others.

Monitoring of all relevant information can easily create large quantities of information to be evaluated. Automated procedures and appropriate tools are recommended in order to distinguish truly significant items from the overall mass of logging information. An analysis of monitoring requirements should be made and the results used to manage the log information to be collected.

Logs of user activities should record the items listed in ISO/IEC 27002:2013, 12.4.1. Logs should be kept for sufficient time in case they are needed for an investigation. They should also be protected in their own right, particularly against unauthorized modification designed to cover up other unauthorized activity (see also 2.8.4.2).

As with all types of incident, system faults can expose vulnerability to loss of service integrity and availability. All faults should be logged to enable orderly corrective action to be taken. In the longer term, logs can be analysed to identify unacceptably unreliable equipment and fault trends in individual devices. The rules for handling reported faults include the review of the fault logs, and the identification of the appropriate corrective action. Special care should be taken where the fault or its correction might have compromised security, and it should be ensured that the corrections achieve their intended goals.

Auditing guidance

For all systems processing information there should be an event log kept that is independent of, and not accessible by, the user. Auditors need to confirm whether the event logging arrangements are appropriate for the security requirements of the organization, and should check the organization's approach to logging. The auditor should check that all records that are required to be kept because of record retention policy, or in order to collect evidence, are properly archived (see also 2.12.1.7): what is recorded, and are the records giving sufficient information?

As a minimum, the log information should identify the event, the person causing the event, changes made, if appropriate, the date and time. In addition, transaction codes, terminal ID, network addresses and actions (such as use of privileges or system utilities, and changes to the configuration of the system) might also be needed. The auditor needs to check what constitutes an event, and check that exceptions are included. The audit needs to check and confirm how long this information is required to be held, in what form and under what protection. Example events include changes made by system administrators and failed logins or access attempts; ask for examples of such event logs.

Event logs need to be reviewed and, where necessary, satisfactory corrective actions should be taken. The auditor needs to check how often the logs are reviewed – the higher the related security risks are, the more frequently the logs should be reviewed. This check should also confirm whether the review process itself is effective and efficient. The principle of separation of duties should be employed in assigning responsibility for reviewing log files; the roles whose activities are being reviewed should not be performing the review.

The logs produced by system monitoring or event logging processes can easily result in large volumes of data. This might result in important information related to security-relevant incidents getting lost in a mass of other less important data. Therefore, tools should be used to filter audit logs with filter rules designed to ensure that all relevant incidents and activities are recognized by such filters. The auditor should enquire about the use and adoption of such tools and review how these tools are applied to detect and react to incidents.

Part of the criteria for review should be that security has not been compromised: check that this is defined in the procedures and understood by management. It should be checked that all faults have been satisfactorily resolved. Auditors should also check that only sufficiently authorized personnel are able to carry out any corrective action, and that these help to avoid recurrence of the faults in the future, and/or sufficiently limit the damage.

2.8.4.2 Protection of log information (ISO/IEC 27001:2013, A.12.4.2)

'Logging facilities and log information shall be protected against tampering and unauthorized access.'

Implementation guidance

The information contained in audit logs, administrator logs, fault logs and logs resulting from monitoring activities is only valuable if its integrity can be relied on. Therefore, it is essential to make the other controls in this control area work to have sufficient protection of log information in place. This is especially important when investigating incidents, or when evidence needs to be provided (see 2.12, particularly 2.12.1.7). The organization should ensure that it is not possible to:

- edit or delete any of the log files, except with explicit authorization;
- modify the type of information being recorded in the logs;
- overwrite logs by using the fact that the storage capacity is limited.

Auditing guidance

Auditors should check the provisions the organization has in place to protect its log information, to ensure that the logging and monitoring controls provide reliable evidence of what is going on in the organization. Check how the logs are stored and maintained, and confirm that they cannot be modified or deleted. Check also who determines what exactly is logged, and confirm that nobody can alter the types of information recorded in the logs or overwrite logs.

2.8.4.3 Administrator and operator logs (ISO/IEC 27001:2013, A.12.4.3)

'System administrator and system operator activities shall be logged and the logs protected and regularly reviewed.'

Implementation guidance

Both automatic and handwritten logs of administrator and user activity are important for providing assurance, through monitoring, of the integrity of computer operation. They are often a very useful aid to incident investigation, and consequently should be protected against alteration by privileged users, ideally by promptly removing them to a log server that is not under the control of the users of the systems generating the log data. Separate detection systems, such as an intrusion detection system, can also be used to monitor user activities.

Log data should be retained for a reasonable period of time and be subject to regular, independent reviews against operating procedures. The logs should identify the time when an event occurred, provide information about the event, and identify the person(s) and processes that were involved in the event.

Auditing guidance

The computer operating procedures should identify the administrator and user logs that need to be kept, both for normal operations and fault incidence. There should be evidence that these logs are independently reviewed as part of internal monitoring. The auditor should check that the logs contain sufficient information, and that they are protected from tampering and deletion, especially by privileged users of the systems creating the logs.

When checking operating logs for context, the auditor should check how shift changes are recorded, the occurrence of carry-over operations, special requirements, etc. Look also at the archiving of logs, both manually and machine recorded: are they identified? Can they be retrieved? Are they protected from unauthorized changes and viewing?

2.8.4.4 Clock synchronisation (ISO/IEC 27001:2013, A.12.4.4)

'The clocks of all relevant information processing systems within an organization or security domain shall be synchronised to a single reference time source.'

Implementation guidance

Most output from computers and communications equipment is time and date stamped. This information will form part of the audit trail for transactions moving between computers. It might also be required in investigations or to resolve disputes and should therefore be entirely consistent between all devices within the scope of the ISMS (see also 2.12.1.7). An internal reference time source should be identified, documented and implemented. The use of an external reference time source should be considered, and the decision on this matter clearly documented. Radio receivers are available that will provide a computer with a signal from an atomic clock and maintain accuracy to the second.

Auditing guidance

The organization needs to establish what its base time shall be; for most this will be local time, but for international organizations some other base may be used, e.g. Greenwich Mean Time (GMT)/Universal Mean Time (UMT). Without proper timing across all systems, audit and monitoring logs can be inaccurate and hence compromised. Any system audit trails and monitoring investigations will rely on accurate system clocks. The auditor needs to check that access to configuration of system clocks is restricted to avoid compromise. There should be some facility to monitor system clocks and correct them, if necessary. Also check what is done to ensure the consistency of wall clocks, which may be used for manual logging, e.g. goods received and incident reports. Ensure that these are used, rather than users' wristwatches; are they in the right place? Can system clocks be used instead?

The auditor needs to check how the transitions to and from British Summer Time (BST) are controlled. What arrangements are made to correlate the time for systems that are located in different time zones? Are any additional checks carried out when portable/mobile devices log into the network?

Finally, the auditor should confirm that other systems, such as CCTV systems, are also using the same reference time source.

2.8.5 Control of operational software (ISO/IEC 27001:2013, A.12.5)

Objective: To ensure the integrity of operational systems.

2.8.5.1 Installation of software on operational systems (ISO/IEC 27001:2013, A.12.5.1)

'Procedures shall be implemented to control the installation of software on operational systems.'

Implementation guidance

Operational systems are vulnerable to the installation of unauthorized software and unauthorized changes to operational software with a resulting loss of system and data integrity. Controls are necessary to reduce the risk of system failure, the introduction of any unauthorized software, and the possibility of fraud. All software updates should be subjected to change control and authorized and tested prior to implementation, and all changes should be logged. Backups of old configurations should be retained and a fallback strategy should be in place for the case of failure of the new system.

New products should be obtained against a business requirement and appropriately authorized. Ensure that valid licences are provided to cover the extent of use intended. For vendor-supplied software, it should be ensured that support is available at the level needed by the organization, and that this support does not cease as long as the organization uses the software.

Auditing guidance

Auditors should check the controls applied for the implementation of software on operational systems: how is the code held on the system? Is source code included? How are new versions introduced? How are system files and libraries protected? What records are kept of changes? Are changes only made if there are business requirements to do so and after security considerations have been made? Developers and maintenance staff need to be aware of the potential dangers of introducing untested code, or of allowing unauthorized code, onto operational systems – check that this awareness exists.

Next, the auditors can check the implementation: what protection is applied to source and object code? What testing stages have to be completed before new or modified code is introduced? Is regression testing adequate? Can previous issues of code be reinstalled? Are full data backups performed before changes, and are fallback arrangements in place in case changes are not successful?

The auditor needs to check the records of changes to operational code: are they complete and sufficiently descriptive and do they show proper authorization? Complex or critical operations can require carefully thought-out and detailed plans for the introduction of new or modified code – look for examples of this.

2.8.6 Technical vulnerability management (ISO/IEC 27001:2013, A.12.6)

Objective: To prevent exploitation of technical vulnerabilities.

2.8.6.1 Management of technical vulnerabilities (ISO/IEC 27001:2013, A.12.6.1)

'Information about technical vulnerabilities of information systems being used shall be obtained in a timely fashion, the organization's exposure to such vulnerabilities evaluated and appropriate measures taken to address the associated risk.'

Implementation guidance

More and more attacks on organizations' information systems are based on the exploitation of published technical vulnerabilities, and the time frame of these attacks gets shorter and shorter. Therefore, the organization should have procedures in place to identify any technical vulnerabilities of its information systems in a timely way and to identify and implement the appropriate reaction to such vulnerabilities.

The necessary roles and responsibilities for this process should be identified, as well as a timeline for the actions to be taken, to ensure that the right actions are taken within the appropriate time.

If a vulnerability has been identified, the organization should identify the risks related to this particular vulnerability, and the suitable action to be taken, e.g. to install or not to install a patch to protect against the vulnerability. If the decision is that a patch should be installed, the organization should ensure that it is tested prior to installation, and there should be rollback procedures in place to go back to the previous state if the patch causes unforeseen problems after being installed. Control 12.6.1 of ISO/IEC 27002:2013 describes the management process for technical vulnerabilities that organizations should consider.

How an organization approaches the problem of technical vulnerabilities is dependent on its need for robust information processing systems and the resources and technical expertise the organization has in place to evaluate patches before installation. Small organizations might restrict their actions to being aware of all relevant patches and installing them in a timely way (possibly taking account of the experiences other organizations have had), whereas larger organizations might include extensive testing before the patches are installed. Whatever approach the organization is taking, it should be based on a risk assessment that takes account of the requirements for resilience to attacks, and the resources the organization has available to address this problem.

Auditing guidance

The auditor should check how the organization is addressing the issues of published technical vulnerabilities. The organization should have assessed the risks associated with published technical vulnerabilities, identified its requirements to protect against attacks exploiting technical vulnerabilities, and put an appropriate management process for technical vulnerabilities in place.

Depending on the requirements of the organization and the resources available, the auditor should check that a sound management process for technical vulnerabilities has been implemented. ISO/IEC 27002:2013, 12.6.1 describes what should be addressed in such a management process.

The correct working of this process should be monitored, and the organization should have procedures in place to evaluate the effectiveness of its technical vulnerability management. Whatever is done in response to identified technical vulnerabilities needs to link in with the change control process that is in place (see 2.10.2.2), and there should always be the option to uninstall a patch and return to the previous state.

2.8.6.2 Restrictions on software installation (ISO/IEC 27001:2013, A.12.6.2)

'Rules governing the installation of software by users shall be established and implemented.'

Implementation guidance

It is now common for certain groups of users to have increased privileges allowing them to install software as necessary for their role; for example, some users may be developing software, and need to install both it and other tools on development systems. Equally, certain software requires users to have the right to install applications in order to update it. In all cases, the use of these privileges should be strictly controlled and appropriate uses documented and monitored.

Auditing guidance

The auditor should ask for and check documentation relating to the authorization of users to install programs (this should apply to administrative users if not to other users), and acceptable uses for these privileges. Permitted categories of software that specific roles are allowed to install (e.g. patches) should be documented, as well as forbidden categories (e.g. software from dubious sources, games and vulnerability analysis tools).

2.8.7 Information systems audit considerations (ISO/IEC 27001:2013, A.12.7)

Objective: To minimize the impact of audit activities on operational systems.

2.8.7.1 Information systems audit controls (ISO/IEC 27001:2013, A.12.7.1)

'Audit requirements and activities involving verification of operational systems shall be carefully planned and agreed to minimise disruptions to business processes.'

Implementation guidance

Prior to any audit of information systems taking place, the audit requirements should be assessed and, if an audit is required, this audit should be carefully planned and a schedule agreed. Audit activity on operational systems might require the use of special programs that access data files used by the system or its applications. Such use should be planned to avoid causing problems and disruption in operational systems. Audit plans should be documented and authorized. ISO/IEC 27002:2013, 12.7.1 gives further guidance on conducting information systems audits.

Auditing guidance

Information systems audit controls and tools used in the audit should not compromise either the information or operations being checked. Where audits are planned, check that the requirements have been identified and appropriate authorization has been obtained from operational management. No information should be changed for the purpose of these activities and access to information should be logged as for any other operation.

The auditor should also check that the interruptions to business activities are minimized. Make sure the audit results are kept and that use of any tools is properly recorded. A check can also be made that any tools are themselves formally validated before use. This includes checking that the person carrying out the audit is independent of the activities being audited.

2.9 Communications security (ISO/IEC 27001:2013, Clause A.13)

2.9.1 Network security management (ISO/IEC 27001:2013, A.13.1)

Objective: To ensure the protection of information in networks and its supporting information processing facilities.

2.9.1.1 Network controls (ISO/IEC 27001:2013, A.13.1.1)

'Networks shall be managed and controlled to protect information in systems and applications.'

Implementation guidance

Networks are especially vulnerable to misuse and abuse, as well as unauthorized access or the unintentional failings of technology. They are complex and it is easy to make mistakes in their configuration, control and protection.

As a result, network integrity can be impaired and availability lost. The confidentiality and integrity of information passing over public networks should also be considered, with the implementation of appropriate controls to protect the information and the organization's connected networks and systems, and the information held in these systems.

The only way to reduce these risks is to put in place effective management and security controls together with sound procedures. Good network security begins with network planning, and security should be

considered throughout design, implementation, operation, problem
management and monitoring. The management of network information
security has become a significant part of the overall security management
activity within an organization, with specialist knowledge being required
for each communications technology. There are also many security tools
available to protect the network in different ways, and their use should
be properly planned:

- remote control of network equipment and user workstations for
  problem solving and software management;
- network monitors (known as 'sniffers') to detect attacks and analyse
  traffic;
- encryption of transmitted data to retain confidentiality;
- restricted routing per user or network address;
- access control techniques to allow only authorized users;
- controls to assure data integrity.

Many of these controls require policies and procedures to be established
at the organizational level. All these techniques require comprehensive
authorized documentation for network designs, implementation,
operation, and changes and monitoring. Constant monitoring of the
activities in the network and security status is essential, with appropriate
records being kept of faults, problems and corrective actions.

Auditing guidance

Network topology and operating environments, particularly where
sensitive traffic is involved, should be properly planned and managed.
The auditor needs to confirm that management has done this, and that
formal records of these activities are available. Have due consideration
and protective mechanisms been employed where networks have access
to or use public networks?

For large, complex operations, use of suitable consultants might be
appropriate; if not, look carefully at the qualifications of internal
network designers. Have the most exposed aspects of network operations
been identified? What protective measures have been adopted? Security
breaches on networks are not always immediately obvious; data might be
intercepted, copied or modified without any apparent trace.

The auditor needs to check what monitoring activities are used to
identify such breaches, and to confirm that the incident reporting
procedures cover this (see also 2.12). Network technology, data
encryption, digital signatures, etc. are all areas of rapid technological
change; the auditor needs to check how the organization is monitoring
the developments in these areas and identifying new threats to security
and existing protection mechanisms.

2.9.1.2 Security of network services (ISO/IEC 27001:2013, A.13.1.2)

'Security mechanisms, service levels and management requirements of all network services shall be identified and included in network services agreements, whether these services are provided in-house or outsourced.'

Implementation guidance

The use of third-party supplied network services can increase the chances of unauthorized access attempts by other parties, leading to breaches of confidentiality and loss of integrity if the third-party services are not sufficiently secure. Availability should also be given special attention, checking on the resilience of the supplier's failover provisions in the event of power, connection or equipment failures. The organization should establish security standards, which will be maintained when the supplier is experiencing or recovering from a failure, and which should identify the security features, service levels and controls required for the services needed. This is best done by considering the detailed security arrangements being offered in a risk assessment. The organization should ensure that the identified security features are provided, and include the identified security requirements in the agreement with the service provider (see also 2.11.1.2). Additional controls might be needed in some circumstances to offset any identified weakness.

Auditing guidance

Where the organization is dependent on external suppliers for any networked services, it is essential that the full extent of all security features, services levels, controls and management requirements are understood. The auditor needs to confirm that the organization has assessed the risks and the needs for security services, that the organization has obtained information about the security features from the service provider, and that the organization has verified that these security features are sufficient and relevant to the identified needs.

The auditor should also check that these security features have been incorporated into operational procedures and security controls, and that there are procedures in place to review and verify security features regularly. The auditor needs to confirm that the organization has covered all aspects of information security, i.e. confidentiality, integrity and availability, in its considerations.

2.9.1.3 Segregation in networks (ISO/IEC 27001:2013, A.13.1.3)

'Groups of information services, users and information systems shall be segregated on networks.'

Implementation guidance

Networks are always vulnerable to unauthorized access attempts, which can result in breaches of confidentiality and loss of integrity for the network or its attached systems. The bigger the network, the greater the risk. Security is easier to manage if the network is divided up into physical or logical domains. Tight security can then be provided to manage the gateways or 'firewalls' between the domains. A firewall can also be used to protect the organization's networks from unauthorized external access, while still allowing public access to the organization's web server, and allowing staff to receive email from other organizations.

Network modelling should be used to design the individual domains and risk assessment will determine the level of security needed to be applied to each domain. Network connection and routing controls should be implemented to achieve sufficient segregation of networks.

The domains and their relationships should be carefully documented. The network security plan should be specific about which systems and network devices are in which domain. It is possible for different parts of a single system to be in more than one domain, e.g. by department or business unit. Provided that the security system keeps them apart logically, this may be acceptable.

Auditing guidance

The larger a domain, the more difficult it can be to secure. This is true of networks as much as any other structure. It is highly likely that secure networks will need access to wider aspects of corporate operations – email, intranet web pages, networks of other organizations, etc. – so separation of particularly sensitive areas is needed.

Appropriate segregation in networks can be achieved by physically segmenting networks or by applying network connection and routing controls, e.g. via bridges, routers and firewalls.

The auditor should check what network domains have been put in place by the organization, that they are appropriate for the security requirements, how they are defined and incorporated into network operations, and how the connection from one network domain to another is controlled. Considering that security domains can impose restrictions in operational performance, the auditor should confirm that these considerations have not led to any compromises in the security of the protected areas.

Where wireless networks are part of the scope of the ISMS, the auditor should check that a risk assessment has been carried out to determine whether direct connection between the wireless network and the main network is appropriate, and that this has identified and implemented all relevant controls to manage the risks. The organization should follow the latest security standards when implementing any wireless network, especially if it is directly connected to the main network.

2.9.2 Information transfer (ISO/IEC 27001:2013, A.13.2)

Objective: To maintain the security of information transferred within an organization and with any external entity.

2.9.2.1 Information transfer policies and procedures (ISO/IEC 27001:2013, A.13.2.1)

'Formal transfer policies, procedures and controls shall be in place to protect the transfer of information through the use of all types of communication facilities.'

Implementation guidance

The exchange of information using electronic communication facilities, such as networks, landline telephones or mobile phones, answering machines, video conferencing or fax machines, carries a lot of risks for compromise of this information. Therefore, the organization should have an information exchange policy and supporting procedures in place describing the rules to be applied when exchanging information. When developing this policy and the supporting procedures, the items listed in control 13.2.1 of ISO/IEC 27002:2013 should be considered.

An appropriate policy dealing with these issues should be communicated to all employees who use any form of information exchange, and awareness training with real-life examples should be used to illustrate the risks involved.

All personnel should be aware of this policy and the related procedures, and when exchanging information they should also be aware of the possibilities of:

- information being compromised if sent to the wrong address in a network;
- information being accessed by unauthorized people if sent unprotected;
- information being compromised through the use of insufficiently protected wireless communication;
- information being compromised when left unattended in printers or fax machines;
- being overheard when using mobile phones in public places;
- sensitive or confidential information being intercepted when communicated;

- messages and faxes being received by the wrong person through misdialling;
- the wrong person picking up a fax or listening to an answering machine message, despite the right number being dialled.

Auditing guidance

The auditor should check that the organization has a policy for information exchange and supporting procedures in place, and that the policy and the procedures address the different types of exchange that are used within the organization. It should be checked, either through procedures or through technical means, that information exchange violating the policy is not permitted. It should also be checked that the policy and the supporting procedures cover all forms of communication facilities, including networks, mobile computing devices, landline telephones and mobile phones, fax machines, handheld computers and answering machines.

Auditors should enquire into the procedures that have been developed to manage such information exchange, and should review these against the items described in ISO/IEC 27002:2013, 13.2.1. The organization should log the information exchange that is taking place, and somebody should have the responsibility to review these logs.

The auditor needs to confirm that employees are aware of these procedures, for example, by asking them about their use of email, wireless communications, mobile phones, answering machines or fax machines, to find out whether they are aware of the risks involved.

2.9.2.2 Agreements on information transfer (ISO/IEC 27001:2013, A.13.2.2)

'Agreements shall address the secure transfer of business information between the organization and external parties.'

Implementation guidance

When sending information to another organization, there is always the risk that it might be compromised in transit. The other organization might have different standards, or different interpretations of labels and the necessary protection. This can lead to unauthorized exposure and a breach of confidentiality, and other forms of compromises of information security, possibly resulting in bad publicity for your organization.

Agreements or contracts should specifically establish the level of security expected to be applied while passing sensitive information to or from a third party, including specific controls (see ISO/IEC 27002:2013, 13.2.2 for more detail on items to be considered).

Agreements should be authorized at an appropriate level in the organization and periodically reviewed. Changes in practice should always be controlled and reflected where necessary in the agreement.

Auditing guidance

Auditors need initially to check which organizations are involved in the transfer of sensitive information, and then to confirm that the necessary contractual documents exist and that these documents address the correct treatment of sensitive and confidential information in transit. This covers not only information but also software. For example, this could be the case where a software house has developed programs for handling critical data and the organization might need to ensure access to that software via escrow agreements.

The auditor needs to check what the organization has done to find out about the protection the other organizations apply for sending and receiving information, and how the organization has addressed situations where protection requirements and controls differ. The auditor needs to check whether agreements between organizations exchanging sensitive information or software are in place and whether these include the items addressed in ISO/IEC 27002:2013, 13.2.2.

2.9.2.3 Electronic messaging (ISO/IEC 27001:2013, A.13.2.3)

'Information involved in electronic messaging shall be appropriately protected.'

Implementation guidance

Email provides a wide variety of information security risks to any organization, if used without appropriate controls. Case history shows that organizations can be open to libel writs as a result of what their staff have written in an email message, often informally and supposedly for internal distribution only. Email messages may also be covered by freedom of information and data protection legislation.

Organizations should have a clear communications policy and approval processes in place regarding the use of electronic messaging. The legal implications of both internal and external messages should be properly understood. The exposure of even an internal message that is critical of another organization or person could result in legal action. An external message might amount to an unintended contract between the parties. Deleted messages might well remain for one or more years in the backup system from which they could be retrieved if required. The courts and statutory regulators have the powers to demand extensive disclosure from archives.

Email can be a major source of infection by malware, via attachments or via links to websites that install malware without the knowledge of the user by taking advantage of vulnerabilities in web browsers, and appropriate controls should be applied to protect against these threats (see also 2.8.2.1). Additionally, an out-of-date email program can permit infection by a maliciously crafted email without the user needing to open the email or any attachments.

Email is also commonly used in attempted financial fraud, to which employees may fall victim.

All these aspects make email a relatively high-risk service. It is essential that staff are properly trained in the organization's requirements and control mechanisms.

Auditing guidance

Using electronic messaging is now very common in almost all organizations. As this form of communication is extremely vulnerable, the controls in place to protect it should be carefully considered. The auditor needs to check the organization's security arrangements for this type of communication, asking, typically, questions such as: how is information included in, and attached to, electronic messages controlled? How is correct receipt verified? How is incoming data verified as to source and integrity? If applicable, what encryption methods are applied? If encryption and digital signatures are used, are the controls discussed in 2.6.1 applied to ensure sufficient security? Is information received from electronic messages checked for virus infection before use? Does an electronic message sent within the organization have a different integrity status from that sent externally and, if so, how is this defined and monitored?

There are considerable legal risks in the use of electronic messaging and organizations should have a clear and implemented policy on this issue. Internal messages could inadvertently be sent to external parties, contracts can be implied, and messages and any attachments could be held on backup for years. Standard disclaimers attached to electronic messages might help but their legal status as protection is not clear.

Auditors should check the organization's security arrangements where access to external messaging services is permitted, and that an appropriate risk assessment has been performed and managed. For example, it might be appropriate to restrict access to message transmission to a limited number of individuals. If so, how is this enforced? Test protection mechanisms.

2.9.2.4 Confidentiality or non-disclosure agreements (ISO/IEC 27001:2013, A.13.2.4)

'Requirements for confidentiality or non-disclosure agreements reflecting the organization's needs for the protection of information shall be identified, regularly reviewed and documented.'

Implementation guidance

Suitable confidentiality agreements should be in place before giving access to confidential information. This should be ensured for all employees of the organization, as well as any relevant external personnel, and any other organization with which information is exchanged. The organization should develop confidentiality agreements that address its particular requirements; examples of what might be included in the confidentiality agreements are given in ISO/IEC 27002:2013, 13.2.4. However, it is most important that this is not used as a definitive list, but only as a starting point.

Requirements for confidentiality agreements can be identified by looking at the following:

*   identified legal, regulatory and contractual requirements – if these requirements impose confidentiality, e.g. as data protection legislation does for personal data, confidentiality agreement(s) might be useful;
*   information exchanged with other organizations – confidentiality agreements with these organizations should be in place to ensure that the confidentiality of the information exchanged is not compromised;
*   asset valuation – whenever the results of the asset valuation have shown that an asset has particular confidentiality requirements, all people having access to the asset should sign a confidentiality agreement;
*   unplanned access to confidential information – it might be the case that people in the organization get unplanned access to confidential information, such as cleaning personnel in an office where the desk has not been cleared. As the requirements for confidentiality agreements may change, it is important that a defined review process is in place that identifies new requirements and ensures that these requirements are addressed in the relevant confidentiality agreements.

Auditing guidance

Auditors should confirm that confidentiality agreement(s) are in place and check whether they address the identified business, legal and contractual and information security requirements. It might be helpful to consult the risk assessment results and see how these link into the different clauses of the confidentiality agreement(s) in place. Auditors should also check that any confidentiality agreement uses legally enforceable terms, so it is of use in disputes that might arise, and that the confidentiality agreements are not in conflict with any existing applicable legislation and regulations.

The auditor needs to confirm that there are defined review and updating procedures in place for each of the confidentiality agreements, and there should be processes in place that ensure that appropriate confidentiality agreements are signed before access to any confidential information is given (see also 2.3.1.2).

2.10 System acquisition, development and maintenance (ISO/IEC 27001:2013, Clause A.14)

2.10.1 Security requirements of information systems (ISO/IEC 27001:2013, A.14.1)

Objective: To ensure that information security is an integral part of information systems across the entire life cycle. This also includes the requirements for information systems which provide services over public networks.

2.10.1.1 Information security requirements analysis and specification (ISO/IEC 27001:2013, A.14.1.1)

'The information security related requirements shall be included in the requirements for new information systems or enhancements to existing information systems.'

Implementation guidance

Information security requirements and vulnerabilities should be recognized from the first stages of information systems' acquisition or development, and all relevant requirements for information security should be specified along with the functional requirements. The development or acquisition of information systems should follow a well-specified and documented procedure that ensures that all identified security requirements are addressed. The requirements analysis should refer to the results of risk assessments, and testing should be used to validate that the developed or purchased information system satisfies the identified requirements. ISO/IEC 27002:2013, 14.1.1 contains a useful list of specific subjects to consider.

Auditing guidance

Organizations should be able to demonstrate to the auditor that information security requirements for the existing and new information systems have been identified and taken into account for the development and acquisition of applications and new systems, and enhancements and upgrades to systems. This really falls into two categories: those where bespoke applications software is developed specifically either for, or by, the organization, or where commercial off-the-shelf (COTS) software is acquired for use in a secure environment. (Note that insecure COTS software might comprise the entire application, or a component which is built into it.)

The organization's analysis of requirements should identify information security requirements (e.g. preservation of integrity within a given application) and these should be considered in the requirements documents for new systems. It is vital that this process takes place for all developed and purchased information systems. Having confirmed that this is the case, the auditor should check to see how these requirements are monitored and reviewed during system development or acquisition, and installation. The auditor should confirm that testing of the information system takes place, where necessary, to check that the requirements are being met. Any identified deficiencies should be analysed, raised at the appropriate management level and satisfactorily resolved.

2.10.1.2 Securing application services on public networks (ISO/IEC 27001:2013, A.14.1.2)

'Information involved in application services passing over public networks shall be protected from fraudulent activity, contract dispute and unauthorized disclosure and modification.'

Implementation guidance

Controls should be implemented to protect the information involved in applications that use public networks, e.g. for electronic commerce.

ISO/IEC 27002:2013, 14.1.2 provides a range of controls that are applicable, and the organization should consider them and identify those applicable to its way of doing business. For example, the application of cryptographic controls (see also 2.6.1) can achieve protection in several ways:

- encryption can be applied to ensure the confidentiality of information such as billing details, customer information and personal information;

- digital signatures can be applied to ensure the integrity of electronic transactions and to authenticate the partners involved in the transactions;
- encryption and digital signatures can be used to achieve non-repudiation that helps to resolve disputes regarding the occurrence or non-occurrence of events.

When using cryptographic controls, care should be taken that an appropriate policy and key management system is in place, and that these controls conform to any legal requirements (see also 2.14.1.5) that might be applicable.

Any organization providing or using application services over public networks should have a policy in place that describes who is allowed to carry out electronic commerce activities, what each of these employees is authorized to do, and what controls are in place to protect and monitor such activities.

Auditing guidance

Auditors should enquire about the current and future activities within the organization. All activities related to the organization's public use or provision of application services should be reviewed for any security-related aspects. This includes an audit check of the following.

- Is an authorization process in place? Can only those employees within the organization that are authorized carry out activities?
- Is there suitable segregation of duties? Are activities that, in combination, can be used to commit fraud or otherwise compromise legitimate communications segregated or supervised?
- Are appropriate cryptographic controls in place (see also 2.6.1) to ensure the authenticity, integrity and confidentiality of information processed in relation to non-repudiation of actions and events, and is a policy in place to regulate the application of such controls?
- Are appropriate network security controls in place to protect the organization's network and the host used for public application services from attacks that can result from the interconnection with other networks (see also 2.9.1.1)?
- Are procedures applied to achieve appropriate verification of actions, payments, etc.?
- Have actions been taken to arrange sufficient insurance?
- Is sufficient protection given to guard against risks from other security problems that might relate to information involved in the provision of public application services (see also ISO/IEC 27002:2013, 14.1.2)?

2.10.1.3 Protecting application services transactions (ISO/IEC 27001:2013, A.14.1.3)

'Information involved in application services transactions shall be protected to prevent incomplete transmission, mis-routing, unauthorized message alteration, unauthorized disclosure, unauthorized message duplication or replay.'

Implementation guidance

If the organization is using application services transactions (e.g. for online payments), controls should be put in place to protect against the risks associated with them, as listed in the control statement above. The organization should use a risk assessment to identify the level of protection required for information involved in transactions. Control 14.1.3 of ISO/IEC 27002:2013 describes items that should be considered for application services transactions, depending on the concerns of the organization.

As described above in 2.10.1.2, the use of cryptographic controls (encryption for confidentiality and digital signatures for integrity and/or authenticity; see also 2.6.1) can help to achieve the desired level of protection. Particular consideration should be given to compliance with any applicable legal or regulatory requirements in the jurisdiction where the transactions take place.

Auditing guidance

The auditor should check how the organization – if it is using application services transactions – has addressed the issue of identifying and implementing the appropriate level of protection for these transactions. Has the organization carried out a risk assessment? Has this assessment taken account of at least the following issues:

- the use of cryptographic means, i.e. electronic signatures, to ensure the integrity and/or authenticity, and encryption to ensure the confidentiality, of information involved in transactions;
- the secure use of, and communication with, authorities managing certificates for digital signatures;
- verification of who is involved in the transactions and of user credentials;
- the use of secure protocols for the communication;
- ensuring the secure storage of the information involved in transactions;
- ensuring compliance with applicable legislation and/or regulations, depending on the jurisdiction(s) that might be involved in the transaction.

2.10.2 Security in development and support processes (ISO/IEC 27001:2013, A.14.2)

Objective: To ensure that information security is designed and implemented within the development life cycle of information systems.

2.10.2.1 Secure development policy (ISO/IEC 27001:2013, A.14.2.1)

'Rules for the development of software and systems shall be established and applied to developments within the organization.'

Implementation guidance

Where software, services, networks or whole environments are being developed, it is necessary for the organization to consider the information security of these environments to prevent the deliberate or accidental inclusion of inappropriate functionality (or of vulnerabilities), which could be used later in the live system to compromise it, and also to protect the intellectual property of the organization, embodied both in the materials being developed, and in the tools and systems being used in the development. The compromise of a development environment itself may thus impact the confidentiality, availability and integrity not only of that environment, but also of the production environment in the future.

A policy should be implemented to ensure that development is carried out to standards that are suitable to the organization's risk profile. ISO/IEC 27002:2013, 14.2.1 contains a checklist of what should be contained in the secure development policy.

Auditing guidance

The auditor should look for evidence of the use of coding or other relevant standards in the development environment, and ask to see documentation supporting a consistent and suitable approach to the identification and resolution of vulnerabilities. Developers should have training and competence in secure practices, which can usually be ascertained via interview. The auditor should confirm that information security standards not only are used, but also that adherence to them is mandated and checked. Third parties (e.g. external organizations, or contractors) should be required to meet the same rules as internal employees. The auditor should confirm that compliance is formally verified by the organization on a routine basis, and non-compliances by any party followed up and resolved satisfactorily. The auditor should look for records of coding audits, both against standards and to find actual vulnerabilities. Check that these were not performed by the staff who wrote the code in question, and that they were performed by appropriately competent individuals.

2.10.2.2 System change control procedures (ISO/IEC 27001:2013, A.14.2.2)

'Changes to systems within the development lifecycle shall be controlled by the use of formal change control procedures.'

Implementation guidance

A system is always more vulnerable when undergoing changes – even fully authorized changes can have damaging effects. There are risks of loss of data integrity, application unavailability, and possibly exposure of confidential information. Therefore, any changes should only take place in accordance with well-defined procedures and after appropriate authorization has taken place.

Formal control and coordination of all changes should be implemented, together with business and technical authorization for each change at all stages of development – requirement capture, design, code, test, and transition to operational status. Changes should be planned and prepared with appropriate testing and review, and the application and operational change control procedures should be integrated and linked as much as possible. Final testing should be signed off by the business before operational implementation. Control 14.2.2 of ISO/IEC 27002:2013 provides further information about the change control procedures that should be applied.

Auditing guidance

Auditors should check that formal change control procedures are in place for all changes made to applications in the operating and system environment. These procedures might need to be in quality plans rather than standard procedures. The audit should also check that similar procedures exist within support and that, where necessary, they provide for changes to design and requirements documents.

In particular, the auditor should check how changes to online operational (and often critical) systems are handled; these often need to be very carefully and extensively planned. Are sufficient fallback arrangements provided if things go wrong? Support staff access to sensitive parts of the system should be restricted to only that which is necessary – investigate how this is implemented.

The auditor should check that all changes are properly authorized (i.e. that the authorization is from the correct level of management and that operations management is involved), that changes are correctly reviewed and tested, and finally that formal authorization is always given before changes are incorporated.

Changes will often be grouped together and incorporated into a release rather than introduced separately. In this situation, the auditor should look to see that release records correctly identify each of the changes made and check that proper configuration control is applied during all changes, and that correct records of the implemented release are in place.

It is likely that an emergency change procedure is also employed to correct operational system failure situations – check that this also meets all of the above criteria.

2.10.2.3 Technical review of applications after operating platform changes (ISO/IEC 27001:2013, A.14.2.3)

'When operating platforms are changed, business critical applications shall be reviewed and tested to ensure there is no adverse impact on organizational operations or security.'

Implementation guidance

Changes to operating system software should be under control (see also 2.10.2.2). However, the impact of operating platform (e.g. operating system) changes on security in general and on the applications should also be assessed. Where new operating software has been installed, the applications should be reviewed and the whole system should be properly tested to ensure there is no vulnerability to breakdowns, leading to non-availability of service, loss of integrity and compromise of information. Therefore, organizations should have procedures in place for the review of applications after any changes have been made to the operational system, and these procedures should include the identification of any applicable vulnerabilities (see also 2.8.6), and the appropriate reaction to such vulnerabilities.

Auditing guidance

The auditor should confirm whether the organization has a review procedure covering operating system changes and their impact on the applications installed on the operational system. This should occur before the planned installation; if possible, a test installation should be evaluated. This review should include an assessment of the controls planned to be in place after the change – check that they are sufficient for the security requirements.

Auditors should look at the inputs to such reviews, such as manufacturers' data sheets and release notes, evaluation data if available, identified software changes that will be needed – e.g. where a 'workaround' has been applied to operating system defects – and support arrangements.

Outputs from these reviews should include any necessary application changes and a plan for installation of the new operating system version. The version of operating system (plus any patches) should be specified in the configuration records. In some situations, organizations might decide not to upgrade the operating system – an audit should check whether, in these situations, it still has access to the necessary levels of support, and, if not, that this is identified and reacted to in the risk assessment.

2.10.2.4 Restrictions on changes to software packages
(ISO/IEC 27001:2013, A.14.2.4)

'Modifications to software packages shall be discouraged, limited to necessary changes and all changes shall be strictly controlled.'

Implementation guidance

Modern software can be immensely complex and is subjected to control and testing during its development. There is therefore considerable risk in making modifications within the user organization, as such changes might introduce vulnerabilities, leading to a breakdown in its internal controls. Loss of confidentiality, integrity and availability can result from such changes.

Therefore, changes to software packages, especially vendor-supplied software packages, should really only be made if there is an overwhelmingly strong business requirement for such changes. Where changes appear to be essential, a risk assessment should identify the vulnerabilities and compensating controls should be selected. Such changes should be authorized at an appropriate level and subjected to change control procedures. If changes are made, a copy of the original software should be kept, and all changes should be fully documented and tested.

When deciding on changes to vendor-supplied software packages, it should also be taken into account that making such changes might mean that vendor support ceases and that the organization then becomes fully responsible for the maintenance, curation and further development of the software.

Auditing guidance

The auditor should check that any changes to software packages require the use of a properly documented and authorized change control procedure. Any changes should be introduced in a controlled fashion – ensure that changes are required to be fully justified and authorized before implementation. Software packages should only be modified if there is a clear business requirement to do so.

Sometimes changes to code can be made as patches, to be incorporated later into future releases; where this is done, ensure that the patch is correctly removed after the future release is installed and that all necessary documentation is updated (see also 2.8.6). Sometimes organizations may have access to the source code but they are not the design authority; such rights to make modifications should be defined in contracts but make sure that modifications are properly incorporated since, possibly not having full access to design records, these changes might further risk system integrity.

The audit should also look at how previously applied changes are handled when new releases of the program are issued – they might need to be re-applied.

The auditor should confirm that there is a complete history of all changes made and that these records are retained for as long as is required, as well as a copy of the original software. The application should have a defined suite of regression tests that can be used to validate the performance of modified code – look at the control of this. Has the organization considered the use of an external specialist testing body, where appropriate?

2.10.2.5 Secure system engineering principles (ISO/IEC 27001:2013, A.14.2.5)

'Principles for engineering secure systems shall be established, documented, maintained and applied to any information system implementation efforts.'

Implementation guidance

The discipline of security engineering is a relatively mature one, and provides a whole raft of principles and tools that can usefully be applied to the implementation of any information system. It enables security to be designed in from the beginning, which makes information security both cheaper, and more likely to be viable (retrofitted security is never the best plan). It also integrates information security into standard development and implementation activities, which is a critically important approach.

However, security engineering approaches must be tailored to the environment and to the organizational culture. They should also be regularly reviewed to ensure that they are up to date and that they are achieving the desired goal of making information security intrinsic to information system engineering activities.

Auditing guidance

The auditor should check what security engineering principles the organization is using when it designs and creates an information system, where it obtained them, and how it is keeping them up to date. What assessment has been done to verify that the principles are suitable, and are they implemented as described? How are they promulgated to contractors and external parties? There is likely to be a role that has responsibility for security engineering; interview staff with this role to ascertain their level of competence in the field.

2.10.2.6 Secure development environment (ISO/IEC 27001:2013, A.14.2.6)

'Organizations shall establish and appropriately protect secure development environments for system development and integration efforts that cover the entire system development lifecycle.'

Implementation guidance

Where an organization is carrying out development activities, it must have not only policies to support suitable processes (see 2.10.2.1), but also a suitably secure development environment. As with any environment, the risks may come from not only the technology being inappropriately selected and configured, but also the actions of people with access to the environment. It should also be noted that multiple development environments may be required to separate more sensitive work from less sensitive work. The organization may indeed choose to have an entirely segregated environment for every development activity it carries out, to reduce the risks of cross-contamination. In this case, there may be a common set of requirements for each category of environment, to simplify the set-up process. Where the work involves the integration of separate systems, other issues come into play, since the scope of the work, and hence the risks, are inevitably higher. Considerations that should be taken into account are listed in ISO/IEC 27002:2013, 14.2.6.

Auditing guidance

The auditor should ask to see documentation describing the secure development environments in use. They should also ask about principles used to determine the appropriate controls to be applied to each environment, and what (if any) connections may exist between environments. A revealing subject to explore is that of administration: does the design of the development environment take into account the risks posed by any common administration back-end, such as a private administrative network, or authentication service?

The auditor should review designs and implementations against the items in ISO/IEC 27002:2013, 14.2.6, and check that all are covered. Interview users of the environment(s) to see if they are aware of the measures that should be in place, and any behaviours that they are expected to exhibit. What background checks are carried out on staff working in the secure development environment(s)?

2.10.2.7 Outsourced development (ISO/IEC 27001:2013, A.14.2.7)

'The organization shall supervise and monitor the activity of outsourced system development.'

Implementation guidance

Outsourcing of software development includes several risks because of the lack of control during the development process. These risks include a lack of quality in the product, as well as unwanted software, such as covert channels or Trojan code, being integrated in the product. Clear contractual agreements should be used to protect against these risks, to ensure the timely delivery, sufficient quality and reliable functioning of the software, and to identify the intellectual property rights of the work carried out. In addition, checks should be devised (as appropriate and possible) to verify that the development carried out is as specified. These may include testing of deliverables, auditing of the outsourcer's environment, and obtaining evidence to support its compliance with the organization's requirements (e.g. outputs of testing, lists of flaws identified and addressed, and certificates to confirm training of developers in secure development).

Auditing guidance

The auditor should confirm that the risks of outsourcing software development are being considered and assessed by the organization. Ideally, the development environment and processes involved should be inspected and reviewed by the organization and the results can then be checked by the auditor. The auditor should also check that risks associated with such developments are periodically reviewed and that changes to security requirements, controls and responsibilities of both parties relating to such developments and any changed or new risks are covered by contract. The auditor should check that the contract covers:

- conditions to measure the timeliness and quality of developed software, and requirements for the quality of code;
- access rights in case an audit is necessary to ensure quality of work done;
- regulations and agreements defining intellectual property rights (IPR) and ownership of developed software;
- sufficient testing of the functionality of developed code, including checks for viruses, covert channels and Trojan code;
- training requirements for developers.

2.10.2.8 System security testing (ISO/IEC 27001:2013, A.14.2.8)

'Testing of security functionality shall be carried out during development.'

Implementation guidance

Security testing should, of course, be carried out prior to operational implementation (see 2.10.2.9). However, in order to ensure that vulnerabilities and inappropriate functionality (e.g. Trojans) are removed from code as soon as possible, and not left until the end of the development process, systems should also be tested on an ongoing basis.

Auditing guidance

The auditor should check whether records exist of testing of development systems throughout their lifespans. The frequency of testing should have been determined by a risk assessment during the design phase, and should be revisited if there are issues found. Tests may be performed by the team carrying out development in the early stages of work.

2.10.2.9 System acceptance testing (ISO/IEC 27001:2013, A.14.2.9)

'Acceptance testing programs and related criteria shall be established for new information systems, upgrades and new versions.'

Implementation guidance

Introduction of new or upgraded systems requires careful planning. The introduction of new systems, upgrades and new versions of software needs to be very carefully managed to ensure no loss of service or compromise of data occurs where operational systems are concerned.

New systems can bring in unrecognized vulnerabilities. It is important that acceptance criteria are established, and that these criteria are checked and that testing is carried out, before the new system is introduced, to ensure that vulnerabilities are controlled. This control is also applicable where new subsystems and devices are being introduced, and where changes are being made to existing systems.

In particular, any adverse effects on existing systems should be identified and brought under control before acceptance into operational services. It is especially important that new facilities connected to the communications network are properly secured prior to connection. All levels of acceptance testing should be documented and signed off at an appropriate level.

For major new developments, the operations function of the organization, and relevant users, should be consulted at all stages in the development process to ensure the practicality of the proposed security design. Involving users is important, as they need to operate the system securely as part of their work. Appropriate tests should be carried out to confirm that all acceptance criteria are fully satisfied.

Auditing guidance

The auditor should look for clear acceptance criteria that need to be fulfilled prior to implementing new or upgraded systems. New systems or

---

processes need to be thoroughly tested before operational use. What plans are there? Have they been reviewed for adequacy? How have the results been recorded?

Adequate testing usually means more than just testing new functionality: has sufficient consideration been given to regression tests? Has the system response to defective data or false user input been covered? Are access controls fully secure? What about other security controls?

Training might need to accompany system acceptance: has this been catered for? Who has determined its adequacy? Have all necessary personnel been involved, both in the preparation of and receiving of training? Who authorizes final acceptance before operational use? Check this is defined and recorded.

Has user testing investigated whether, and how, users may seek to bypass security measures?

2.10.3 Test data (ISO/IEC 27001:2013, A.14.3)

Objective: To ensure the protection of data used for testing.

2.10.3.1 Protection of test data (ISO/IEC 27001:2013, A.14.3.1)

'Test data shall be selected carefully, protected and controlled.'

Implementation guidance

Test data should normally be fictitious, but there are occasions when operational, tokenized or anonymized operational data needs to be used. The organization is vulnerable to breaches of confidentiality when such data is used and it should avoid such use as far as possible, and control and protect the data to at least the same extent as operational data if its use in tests cannot be avoided.

The use of operational data should be recognized in risk assessments and the higher-security requirements noted in test plans. Each instance of use should be authorized, and the same level of access controls as applied for the operational system should be in place. When the tests have been finalized and the data is no longer needed, it should be erased immediately and securely from the test system.

Auditing guidance

The auditor needs to confirm, by means of appropriate evidence, that data used for testing is properly controlled. Tests should be reproducible and so the data used should be distinct and available for any retesting. Use of live data for testing should be discouraged and, if used, it should be modified to remove any personal or otherwise sensitive information.

This is not always completely possible – or not possible to completely assure – so check how this is handled and how any results of the testing – data files, logs, debug files, caches and recorded results – are protected.

Use of live data for testing should be properly authorized on each occasion – check that this is done. Check also that there is a method to completely remove any data put into live databases during testing, and verify the access controls in place. Access to test application systems should be as tightly controlled as access to operational systems. All actions carried out during the tests should have been logged – check that these logs exist, and use them as evidence of how test data is handled and protected.

2.11 Supplier relationships (ISO/IEC 27001:2013, Clause A.15)

2.11.1 Information security in supplier relationships (ISO/IEC 27001:2013, A.15.1)

Objective: To ensure protection of the organization's assets that are accessible by suppliers.

2.11.1.1 Information security policy for supplier relationships (ISO/IEC 27001:2013, A.15.1.1)

'Information security requirements for mitigating the risks associated with supplier's access to the organization's assets shall be agreed with the supplier and documented.'

Implementation guidance

There are several ways suppliers can cause risks to the organization's information and information processing facilities. This might be via physical access as well as via logical access, e.g. using online connections, or remote working with the organization's assets.

If an organization intends to allow suppliers to have access to sensitive data or to secure environments, it needs to have an overarching policy covering what any supplier must and must not do, and should also have a master list of suppliers. The risks that apply to each working relationship with suppliers need to be identified and assessed.

To manage the implementation of this policy, the organization should create a standard process and procedure for managing supplier security, tailored to the security level of the information to which the supplier will be exposed.

Auditing guidance

The auditor should confirm that there are a set of principles and a top-level policy and procedure for handling supplier security. ISO/IEC 27002:2013, 15.1.1 contains a list of the types of information that should be in the policy. The auditor should also check that risk assessments are carried out to assess the risks related to suppliers.

Ask for a master list of suppliers, which should indicate the security level of the information to which each supplier is authorized to be exposed, and should also reference the specific agreements made with that supplier (see 2.11.1.2).

2.11.1.2 Addressing security within supplier agreements (ISO/IEC 27001:2013, A.15.1.2)

'All relevant information security requirements shall be established and agreed with each supplier that may access, process, store, communicate, or provide IT infrastructure components for, the organization's information.'

Implementation guidance

The same level of security as applies to the organization's staff should be provided for supplier staff, including user IDs, passwords, data access controls and physical security. This should be ensured when supplier personnel access assets on the organization's side, as well as when the supplier processes information or uses information processing facilities on its site. What needs to be taken into account when developing the agreement that regulates the supplier access is that the organization is not in charge of the supplier's management, personnel controls, IT and security policies and practices. The other organization might also have a quite different set of ethics and business culture. These differences should be identified and assessed, perhaps before deciding to do business with the other party.

The key control that needs to be in place before anything else happens is the contract or agreement. This should spell out in appropriate detail the controls to be exercised. It should also provide extensive details on the IT facilities that each party will make available to the other and the security controls to be put in place. Suppliers should not be given access to the organization's information and/or information processing facilities until the appropriate controls have been implemented.

The implementation guidance of ISO/IEC 27002:2013, 15.1.2 provides a list of suggested items that should be put in place as required by the results of the risk assessment. The contract or agreement clauses could also require compliance with ISO/IEC 27001:2013, or even certification, again depending on the requirements. Ensure that the signatories on both sides are properly identified and authorized.

The security documentation set should include copies of all relevant contracts or agreements and, possibly, several additional documents describing specific elements of the relationship. It might be helpful to include security controls, policies and procedures in a security plan that can be given to the third party. Any deviation from these requirements should be justified and documented.

Auditing guidance

The auditor should check the results of the risk assessment the organization has carried out for each supplier. Risks might result from remote access to mainframe or server software, or from the internet connection and intranets that might not be as isolated as they first appear, particularly where multiple sites are involved, as well as from physical access.

The auditor should also check that all security requirements and risks regarding supplier arrangements are identified and addressed in a formal contract or service level agreement between the two organizations. The implementation guidance of ISO/IEC 27002:2013, 15.1.2 provides a list of issues that should be considered for inclusion in such agreements. The auditor should check that the organization has adequate procedures in place to ensure that all security issues are addressed prior to giving a supplier access to any of the organization's assets.

It is also necessary to ensure that suppliers are actually aware of all the security arrangements they have to put in place, and understand and agree what these arrangements involve. An example could be to ask the supplier about its compliance with ISMS standards, or ask for its ISMS certification. The auditor should also ask the organization how the agreements cover the situation where a supplier does not perform in accordance with the expectations of the organization. The auditor should check that all relevant liabilities and potential disruptions have been identified and are addressed appropriately. Provisions need to be in place for modifying agreements, when necessary, as well as for their termination.

2.11.1.3 Information and communication technology supply chain (ISO/IEC 27001:2013, A.15.1.3)

'Agreements with suppliers shall include requirements to address the information security risks associated with information and communications technology services and product supply chain.'

Implementation guidance

Having a relationship with a supplier (e.g. a product vendor, or cloud hosting provider) frequently means that, through them, the organization may be exposed to risks posed by other suppliers to that first-party supplier. For example: the vendor of a piece of technology may outsource maintenance to another company, which operates as a franchise. When specialist advice is required, the franchise staff may bring in staff from the manufacturer.

This chain of suppliers needs to be managed via agreements with the supplier with which the organization has a direct contractual relationship. ISO/IEC 27002:2013, 15.1.3 contains a list of considerations to be taken into account when designing a supplier agreement to manage this 'inherited' risk. The organization should actively investigate its information and communications technology (ICT) supply chain, and identify any increased areas of risk.

One key area is the question of how these suppliers change, and how they are chosen; each link in the chain may do this differently, producing possible gaps in security.

Auditing guidance

The auditor should ask to review supplier agreements, and compare them against the list in ISO/IEC 27002:2013, 15.1.3. Are all relevant topics taken into account? Has a risk assessment been carried out on all supply chains? Have appropriate controls been identified and implemented? How is their effectiveness assessed? The auditor should look for unexpected supply chains, such as those related to disposal of sensitive waste.

2.11.2 Supplier service delivery management (ISO/IEC 27001:2013, A.15.2)

Objective: To maintain an agreed level of information security and service delivery in line with supplier agreements.

2.11.2.1 Monitoring and review of supplier services (ISO/IEC 27001:2013, A.15.2.1)

'Organizations shall regularly monitor, review and audit supplier service delivery.'

Implementation guidance

Once the operations of the service provider have started, it is up to the organization to ensure that the services delivered conform to the requirements specified in the contract. One of the most important means to ensure that security controls, service definitions and service delivery levels are provided as specified by the supplier (see 2.11.1.2) is to monitor and review these controls and services. This can include checking fairly obvious issues, such as the availability levels of the provided service, or it can be something more involved to be checked, such as the security controls the service provider has agreed to in the contract to provide for the organization's information. Therefore, the organization should put responsibilities and procedures in place to monitor service delivery and to review service reports produced by the supplier. ISO/IEC 27002:2013, 15.2.1 provides a list of activities that the supplier service management process should include.

Another issue to be monitored and reviewed is what the supplier does to manage information security incidents. It should be stated in the contract or agreement that the supplier will provide the organization with information about information security incidents, and the organization should have assigned responsibilities, sufficient resources and procedures in place to review these reports and to verify that the supplier handles these issues sufficiently well. The same is true for any other problems, faults, events, etc. that might happen and could have an impact on the organization's information or the services provided to the organization.

If the agreement or contract allows audits to take place, then this is another way the organization can verify that the supplier acts in accordance with the contract or agreement. The organization should have the following in place to ensure that the relevant information is obtained:

- ensuring that all relevant reports, records, audit logs, etc. are received from the supplier;
- having procedures in place, responsibilities assigned and sufficiently qualified personnel and other resources available to review the reports, records and logs;
- being able to react to any findings, nonconformities or security problems the supplier has not adequately dealt with.

Auditing guidance

The auditor should look for evidence that the organization is receiving all relevant reports, records and logs of services provided, and that the organization has procedures in place to review the reports, records and logs. To check this, the auditor should ask for records or reports provided, and for any records that are produced as a result of the reviewing activity of the organization. These documents should also show that the activities listed in ISO/IEC 27002:2013, 15.2.1 are taking place.

In addition, the auditor should look at records of actions the organization has carried out to check the security controls, service definitions and service delivery levels, to ensure the procedures are applied correctly. The organization should also have procedures in place to react to any nonconformity of the supplier with the requirements specified in the contract or agreement.

The auditor should confirm that the organization has assigned responsibilities for monitoring and review activities, and that the people carrying out review activities have sufficient skills and time available to carry out their review activities.

If the agreement or contract allows the organization to carry out audits of the supplier, it should be established, e.g. by looking at audit reports, that the organization does audit the supplier.

2.11.2.2 Managing changes to supplier services (ISO/IEC 27001:2013, A.15.2.2)

'Changes to the provision of services by suppliers, including maintaining and improving existing information security policies, procedures and controls, shall be managed, taking account of the criticality of business information, systems and processes involved and re-assessment of risks.'

Implementation guidance

It is usual that changes occur in the provision of services by suppliers; a list of possible types of changes is given in ISO/IEC 27002:2013, 15.2.2. The organization should have procedures in place to react to, and to proactively manage, these changes. This includes re-assessing the risks involved in the new arrangements (see 2.11.2.1), negotiating variations to changes, and possibly modifying supplier contracts or entering into new agreements or contracts. It is important that this takes place following a well-defined procedure, and with appropriate authorization.

Particular care should be taken in the case of changes that affect risk levels. If something has changed within the organization, or in the technology used to provide the services, this should initiate a review of the security controls in place, resulting in changes to existing controls to maintain information security risk at an acceptable level.

Auditing guidance

The organization should have procedures in place to manage any changes to services provided by suppliers. The auditor should check that these procedures include the requirement to re-assess the risks, taking account of the possibly changed business requirements and the systems involved. The auditor should also check that the process requires management approval prior to any changes being made, and that all relevant parts of the organization, e.g. roles with responsibility for legal matters, have the opportunity to review changes to the contract or agreement.

2.12 Information security incident management (ISO/IEC 27001:2013, Clause A.16)

2.12.1 Management of information security incidents and improvements (ISO/IEC 27001:2013, A.16.1)

Objective: To ensure a consistent and effective approach to the management of information security incidents, including communication on security events and weaknesses.

2.12.1.1 Responsibilities and procedures (ISO/IEC 27001:2013, A.16.1.1)

'Management responsibilities and procedures shall be established to ensure a quick, effective and orderly response to information security incidents.'

Implementation guidance

Information security incidents can result in breaches of confidentiality, failure of integrity of equipment and data, and, most commonly, loss of availability. They are usually preventable and provide a valuable opportunity to improve procedures and processes to prevent them occurring again. Examples include fire or flood, electrical failure, hardware breakdown, failed software, virus infection, unauthorized access (actual or attempted) to controlled premises or to computer systems, corrupted or lost data, misdirected emails and failure of any security control.

The organization should have procedures in place that ensure the orderly and effective reaction to reported information security events and weaknesses. The procedures should ensure that all reported events are reviewed and investigated, where appropriate, that recovery procedures are triggered, and that roles of suitable seniority are involved in reviews. ISO/IEC 27002:2013, 16.1.1 provides a list of measures that should be applied to properly manage information security incidents.

Auditing guidance

The auditor should check that information security incident management procedures are in place and that they are compatible with the reporting scenarios described in ISO/IEC 27002:2013, 16.1.2. They should also check that all reported information security events and weaknesses are reacted to appropriately. ISO/IEC 27002:2013, 16.1.1 describes the procedures that should be in place to handle and recover from system failures, errors, security breaches, etc. including contingency arrangements and auditing activities.

Auditing guidance

The auditor should confirm that the organization has appropriate procedures and management channels for reporting information security events. Auditors should check that the procedures deal with all possible events and provide an identified point of contact and sufficient response. If an organization claims to have had no events to report, and thus the process cannot be demonstrated, it is probably the case that events and problems took place but no one noticed. The absence of reports does not represent a good sign of a well-functioning information security event reporting procedure.

Everyone in the organization should be aware of their responsibility to report information security events, and they should know who the points of contact are, and what information the reporting form should contain. The auditor should check that the reporting forms are easy to fill in, and support the reporting action.

The auditor should check that the definition of what is and is not an information security event is clearly described and that staff understand this. It could be useful to ask example questions such as: 'Would you consider finding an unattended security safe open a security event?', and 'If somebody reported receiving somebody else's salary slip, would that be considered a security event?'. Obviously such questions need to be applicable in the environment concerned, but answers from staff can be quite revealing and indicate the general approach to such matters. Where reports are present, check the reaction to this event: has it been settled? Have the reasons been investigated? And has the person who provided the original report been informed of the outcome (if this is not confidential)? Are procedures in place to address failure to report information security events?

2.12.1.3 Reporting information security weaknesses (ISO/IEC 27001:2013, A.16.1.3)

'Employees and contractors using the organization's information systems and services shall be required to note and report any observed or suspected information security weaknesses in systems or services.'

Implementation guidance

Any organization will always be vulnerable to the exploitation of unrecognized security weaknesses. No system can be 100 per cent secure. Because of their knowledge of how the security controls, systems and software work, many IT staff are in a very good position to recognize weaknesses in security. They should be encouraged to report their suspicions to allow proper investigation and corrective measures, if necessary. This is, of course, equally true for any other users – if they observe any suspected security weakness in the information systems they are working with they should be obliged to report any such weaknesses immediately.

Procedures should require all users to note and report any observed or suspected security weaknesses in, or threats to, security controls, systems or services. Users should report these matters either to their line management, directly to their service provider or to any other defined point of contact, as quickly as possible, where they should be recorded and investigated. They should be aware that they should not try to exploit the identified weaknesses in any way.

Auditing guidance

The auditor should confirm that similar reporting procedures as those for information security events are in place for suspected or real security weaknesses. The reporting process should be easy to use, supported by a good reporting form, making the reporting and provision of relevant information easy, and there should be clearly identified points of contact.

It is important that all employees, contractors and third-party users are aware of the importance of reporting security weaknesses, and that this includes any weaknesses, not just those related to information processing facilities – an open window might also be a security weakness. The procedures for reporting should also include regulations for the employees to not use security weaknesses, e.g. to gain unauthorized access – even if the original intent is just to prove the weakness, this might cause serious damage.

2.12.1.4 Assessment of and decision on information security events (ISO/IEC 27001:2013, A.16.1.4)

'Information security events shall be assessed and it shall be decided if they are to be classified as information security incidents.'

Implementation guidance

Each event that is reported should be reviewed by the person to whom it is reported (the point of contact) to ascertain its level of impact. This should be used to determine whether the event should be classified as an information security incident, and the decision and supporting justification should be recorded on the incident reporting system. This is the initial triage phase of information security incident management, which ensures that the efforts of incident response teams are focused upon the correct events, and that serious incidents are handled promptly. In order to ensure that classification is consistent, the organization should have an approved classification scale, with appropriate supporting guidance; the scale should be periodically reviewed for clarity, relevance and usefulness, and updated as required.

The point of contact may not be the final arbiter of classification; if the organization has a team that handles information security incidents, it should confirm the initial classification.

Auditing guidance

The auditor should ask for records of incidents, and timeline documentation, and check that there is a point where a clear determination is made of whether an event should be classified as an incident. They should ask how this was determined; guidance documentation should be readily available to all points of contact, and a list of points of contact available to all staff. Points of contact should be aware of how to classify an incident. There should also be a process for notifying points of contact should the guidance change.

2.12.1.5 Response to information security incidents (ISO/IEC 27001:2013, A.16.1.5)

'Information security incidents shall be responded to in accordance with the documented procedures.'

Implementation guidance

Information security incidents should be responded to in accordance with management requirements, and as documented (see 2.2.1.1). ISO/IEC 27002:2013, 16.1.5 provides a list of actions that should be carried out to properly manage information security incidents. The organization should nominate a point (or points) of contact, to ensure that a clear reporting line is used.

One particularly important consideration with regard to incident response is that it must be decided very early on whether evidence will need to be collected (see 2.12.1.7). This will shape the whole incident response process.

Auditing guidance

The auditor should confirm that all of the activities described in ISO/IEC 27002:2013, 16.1.5 are properly documented in procedures, that all responsibilities have been identified, that appropriate management control is exercised, and that all information security incidents and their follow-up activities are properly recorded.

2.12.1.6 Learning from information security incidents (ISO/IEC 27001:2013, A.16.1.6)

'Knowledge gained from analysing and resolving information security incidents shall be used to reduce the likelihood or impact of future incidents.'

Implementation guidance

In addition to detecting and taking action to resolve information security incidents, it is important that the organization (and the relevant people within the organization) learns from these incidents to avoid future problems or, if they do occur again, so they can be dealt with more effectively. This is also part of the performance evaluation and improvement aspects of the ISMS (see ISO/IEC 27001:2013, Clauses 9 and 10), as the evaluation of incidents that have taken place helps to identify where the controls do not work as intended, and where improvements are necessary. Learning from information security incidents will provide useful information about actions that need to be taken to enhance security, and suitably anonymized case studies should also be used judiciously in training and awareness programmes.

Auditing guidance

Auditors should review examples of how the organization has reacted to information security incidents, and software and system weaknesses, in the past. They should review how the organization quantifies and measures incidents, and whether the incident management procedures are appropriate for the incidents that have occurred or are likely to occur in the future.

The auditor should check the organization's claims that an insufficient number of incidents have occurred or insufficient information or evidence is available to be learnt from. The auditor should check whether this is a sign that the reporting procedures for information security events and weaknesses are not used or that the process is ineffective. The auditor should carry out a further review in these cases.

The auditor should confirm that a process to react to information security incidents and weaknesses is in place. Such a process should include the implementation of additional controls or procedures to avoid recurrences, to limit the damage, to collect evidence, or to allow a quicker and more efficient reaction in the future. Anonymized incidents should be used in training and awareness programmes to give real-life examples.

2.12.1.7 Collection of evidence (ISO/IEC 27001:2013, A.16.1.7)

'The organization shall define and apply procedures for the identification, collection, acquisition and preservation of information, which can serve as evidence.'

Implementation guidance

It is important that an organization ensures the collection of admissible and complete evidence for any information security incident that takes place, since very often it is not obvious whether an incident might finally result in a court case or not. The organization should have guidelines and procedures for the collection of evidence that ensure appropriate admissibility, quality and completeness of the evidence.

Once evidence is collected, it should be managed and stored securely, to guarantee that no one can modify or destroy it without authorization. It should also be ensured that the evidence is available in a timely manner and in a form that is required by court. Control 16.1.7 of ISO/IEC 27002:2013 describes factors that should be taken into account when writing procedures for the collection of evidence.

If the organization is carrying out any investigative or forensic work, this should only be done using forensically sound copies of any evidence that might be required later, to ensure it can be proved that the actual evidence has not been altered or tampered with.

Auditing guidance

Collection of evidence is important to be able to provide adequate support in legal procedures and actions that might take place as a result of information security incidents, such as breach of civil or criminal law. The auditor should confirm that the organization has procedures in place to collect evidence; auditors should check that these procedures include the considerations in ISO/IEC 27002:2013, 16.1.7 and that they ensure that:

- the information collected conforms to applicable standards or codes of practice for the production of such evidence to be deemed admissible as evidence;
- the quality and completeness of such evidence, i.e. the weight of evidence, is appropriate.

Auditors should check where collected evidence is stored, and whether it is possible for unauthorized persons to modify or destroy such evidence. In addition, auditors should consider the conditions when the collection of evidence needs to be activated. Collection of evidence should start at an early stage to ensure that no information is destroyed.

2.13 Information security aspects of business continuity management (ISO/IEC 27001:2013, Clause A.17)

2.13.1 Information security continuity (ISO/IEC 27001:2013, A.17.1)

Objective: Information security continuity shall be embedded in the organization's business continuity management systems.

2.13.1.1 Planning information security continuity (ISO/IEC 27001:2013, A.17.1.1)

'The organization shall determine its requirements for information security and the continuity of information security management in adverse situations, e.g. during a crisis or disaster.'

Implementation guidance

In the case of any serious, unexpected event, especially one that affects business continuity, it is important that information security does not 'fall by the wayside'. If a level of security is necessary when things are going well, then it is also necessary when things are going wrong – unless the organization wishes to escalate a business continuity event into a combined business continuity event and information security incident.

It is therefore essential that information security is considered and included in the overall business continuity management process. Thus the process that the organization uses to manage and recover from crises (whether it is called the disaster recovery process, the business continuity process, or something else) should have integrated into it the notion and principle that information security should remain important in a crisis, and should make this possible. The organization should identify and document its information security requirements for business continuity. These should be based upon clearly realized and authorized objectives for information security continuity.

If the organization is dependent on the availability and reliability of services provided by a supplier, it should also check the plans that the supplier has put in place to deal with interruptions of its services. The organization should ensure that the levels of information security provided in suppliers' business continuity arrangements are sufficient for its requirements. It might also be worthwhile to test these situations to know what to expect in an emergency case.

Auditing guidance

The auditor should confirm that the organization has a clear statement of its objectives for information security continuity. To support this, the auditor should check that the organization has documentation that pertains to the management of serious adverse events (by whatever name). There should be a policy statement regarding preservation of information security during the management of, and recovery from, these events. There should be evidence of a risk assessment, leading to a list of requirements for information security during an adverse event.

2.13.1.2 Implementing information security continuity
(ISO/IEC 27001:2013, A.17.1.2)

'The organization shall establish, document, implement and maintain processes, procedures and controls to ensure the required level of continuity for information security during an adverse situation.'

Implementation guidance

Business continuity/disaster recovery plans should be designed to achieve the security requirements that have been identified in the risk assessment (see 2.13.1.1). Control 17.1.2 of ISO/IEC 27002:2013 describes the key elements that should be included in the information security continuity management process.

Both information security specialists and business continuity/disaster recovery specialists should be involved in integrating information security continuity into the plans.

Auditing guidance

The plan for handling adverse events should include information security considerations throughout the process, including within the business impact analysis stage. Auditors should confirm that the scope and details of this plan fulfil the organization's information security requirements, and that it has been signed off by management. A list of criteria that such a plan should satisfy is given in ISO/IEC 27002:2013, 17.1.2.

Auditors should check that the timescales associated with the plan are sufficient for the business requirements, and that they are realistic.

Staff responsible for managing crises should have access to (and understand) instructions on how information security should be managed, and staff with information security responsibilities should have access to (and understand) instructions on their responsibilities during a crisis.

In addition, the audit should review that:

- all responsibilities are agreed and assigned;
- all procedures defined in the plans are documented and implemented according to the implementation schedule;
- all staff are aware and understand what they are supposed to do in case of emergencies and business interruptions.

Testing of continuity plans is essential and auditors should determine the testing schedule, which may be defined in the planning framework or the plan(s) itself. It is unlikely that plans with any degree of complexity will work perfectly first time; individuals need to follow the procedures to handle the situation effectively and this will only work if it has been practised.

2.13.1.3 Verify, review and evaluate information security continuity (ISO/IEC 27001:2013, A.17.1.3)

'The organization shall verify the established and implemented information security continuity controls at regular intervals in order to ensure that they are valid and effective during adverse situations.'

Implementation guidance

Whenever anything in the organization changes, for whatever reason (whether as part of a planned change, or as a result of disaster recovery activities), it is important that the appropriate level of information security is maintained and does not get missed out, or left for later. Most importantly, when plans, processes and standards change, information security must also be considered in that particular type of change process. 2.10.2.2 also covers related considerations (change control).

The objectives for information security continuity should be referred to during the change process for any other process or plan, to ensure that information security continuity is maintained. The final state of the process should be checked against the objectives to ensure that the objectives are still met.

Auditing guidance

The auditor should confirm that there is a well-defined plan for information security continuity: a full review of all proposed changes to policies, processes and standards against information security objectives, analysis and review. ISO/IEC 27002:2013, 17.1.3 contains a list of activities the organization should be undertaking; ask for records for these activities. The auditor should look for the results of functionality tests: were any problems encountered, and have these been analysed and corrected? What were the performance measures? Did these meet the service level obligations?

The auditor should be suspicious of plans that have not been regularly updated: are there records to demonstrate that these have been reviewed for compliance with information security continuity requirements? The auditor should check that responsibilities for the maintenance and updating of the plans have been defined, and that any changes to the plans can only be made with appropriate authorization.

2.13.2 Redundancies (ISO/IEC 27001:2013, A.17.2)

Objective: To ensure availability of information processing facilities.

2.13.2.1 Availability of information processing facilities (ISO/IEC 27001:2013, A.17.2.1)

'Information processing facilities shall be implemented with redundancy sufficient to meet availability requirements.'

Implementation guidance

Availability is a core aspect of information security, along with other attributes such as confidentiality and integrity. In order to ensure availability, it is important to identify first what the organization actually requires in terms of recovery times following failure, whether it can tolerate any loss of availability, and what current systems provide. Where these are not in agreement, additional measures (such as redundant equipment) should be implemented to increase availability to match need. Risk assessments of the new architecture should be carried out, to identify and manage any increased risks (for example, from copying data between mirrored systems in geographically separate locations via public networks).

Auditing guidance

The auditor should request documents detailing availability requirements, risk assessments, information regarding redundant systems, testing records, records of recovery times following unplanned loss of availability, and any compensating controls that may have been introduced to address additional risks incurred by the introduction of redundant equipment. The auditor should confirm that the organization has appropriate redundancy arrangements that are sufficient to meet availability requirements.

2.14 Compliance (ISO/IEC 27001:2013, Clause A.18)

2.14.1 Compliance with legal and contractual requirements (ISO/IEC 27001:2013, A.18.1)

Objective: To avoid breaches of legal, statutory, regulatory or contractual obligations related to information security and of any security requirements.

2.14.1.1 Identification of applicable legislation and contractual requirements (ISO/IEC 27001:2013, A.18.1.1)

'All relevant legislative statutory, regulatory, contractual requirements and the organization's approach to meet these requirements shall be explicitly identified, documented and kept up to date for each information system and the organization.'

Implementation guidance

All statutory, regulatory and contractual requirements should be identified and documented by the organization to ensure their fulfilment. The organization should identify the approach to meet all these requirements. Especially when thinking of conducting business in other countries, the identification of applicable legislation should be supported by an expert, e.g. a lawyer. Special attention is required when conducting online business or trading to ensure compliance with all relevant legislation in the countries involved. As the statutory, regulatory and contractual requirements will change over time, it is important that the organization has procedures in place to keep up to date.

Auditing guidance

The organization should present to the auditors the actions that have been taken to identify, document and comply with all applicable statutory, regulatory and contractual requirements. The auditors should check that no applicable legislation, regulations or contracts have been forgotten or missed by mistake. The auditor should confirm that the organization has controls in place to comply with the requirements that have been identified. Responsibilities for these controls should be identified and documented, and those responsible should be aware of their responsibilities. Someone should be responsible for keeping the identified statutory, regulatory and contractual requirements up to date, as these will change over time.

2.14.1.2 Intellectual property rights (ISO/IEC 27001:2013, A.18.1.2)

'Appropriate procedures shall be implemented to ensure compliance with legislative, regulatory and contractual requirements related to intellectual property rights and use of proprietary software products.'

Implementation guidance

Organizations are vulnerable to failure to comply with restrictions on copying copyright material. There is a serious risk of legal action being taken against the organization and individual staff where, for example, software is being used on more than the number of systems for which it is licensed.

The organization should put rules in place for the handling of copyright material, and these rules should take into account all types of copyright material, e.g. software or document copyright, design rights, trademarks, patents, and source code licences. Staff should be made aware of the rules. For software, it is especially important to make staff aware of these rules, and inventory checks should be carried out at least annually to provide assurance that all software in use (that is, software loaded on the system) is properly licensed. Documentary records should be maintained of the inventory of software on each system (see also 2.4.1.1).

Control 18.1.2 of ISO/IEC 27002:2013 provides guidelines on the protection of copyright material. The organization and all staff should be aware that copyright infringement can lead to legal action, which may involve criminal proceedings.

Auditing guidance

Auditors should confirm that the organization has procedures in place to protect the intellectual property rights of copyright information and software. These procedures should describe rules for handling material that is marked as copyright, design rights or trademarks, and employees should be aware of how to handle such material. These rules should address the handling of all copyright material, irrespective of the form it takes. The auditor should confirm that users are aware that any unauthorized use, or copying, of intellectual property rights material or software might lead to legal action.

There should be strict controls on the use of software and other copyrighted material (e.g. subscription-based online content) in the organization. Auditors should investigate what licences have been purchased and then how compliance is maintained. Many commercial packages provide licence agreements on packaging and this comes in various forms – there is no common format for information such as number of users and restrictions to use – therefore, further information needs to be gathered to check that the software is used in compliance with the licensing agreement.

One way to address these issues would be to draw up a table of key resources protected by copyright and then identify the key aspects of each licence together with a record of actual use. The auditor should look for the use of development tools and libraries: have these been used correctly? With bespoke software developed for the organization, look at the development or support contract: is access to source code provided? Can in-house changes be applied? Are there restrictions on the use or location of the software? Ensure that the responsible personnel in the organization are fully aware of their obligations regarding software copyright. The auditor should check desktop computers at random for unlicensed material.

2.14.1.3 Protection of records (ISO/IEC 27001:2013, A.18.1.3)

'Records shall be protected from loss, destruction, falsification, unauthorized access and unauthorized release, in accordance with legislatory, regulatory, contractual and business requirements.'

Implementation guidance

Organizations will have a number of essential documents and records, such as accounting records, database records, transaction logs, audit logs and operational procedures, that need to be retained and should be protected from loss, breach of confidentiality or modification. These items should be listed in the asset inventory (see also 2.4.1.1) and appropriate controls selected and implemented to ensure the protection of these records until the end of their retention period. The continued presence of the items should be confirmed by documented inventory check at least annually.

For example, under various regulations organizations are required to maintain business records of certain types for periods up to 10 years, and an organization is open to prosecution where this is not carried out.

When keeping records for such a long time, due consideration should be given to deterioration of the media on which these records are stored, and it should be ensured that tools (e.g. microfiche readers, software and cryptographic keys) are still available, and it is still possible, to actually access records up to the end of their retention period. Control 18.1.3 of ISO/IEC 27002:2013 provides further guidance on the protection of organizational records.

Auditing guidance

All records required for legal or regulatory purposes are usually a subset of all the records an organization will need to keep for business purposes or other reasons. The auditor should confirm that all records required for legal or regulatory purposes (e.g. financial records, customs records, legal records and environmental records) are identified and that all requirements are complied with.

The exact requirements will vary from country to country and the organization needs to be aware of, and comply with, all applicable requirements. The auditor should check that this has been done and verified by the appropriate personnel. The storage arrangements (including security), and the requirements for review and disposal should all be defined in procedures.

There should be an inventory of records and auditors should check this for accuracy. Some documentation might now be held electronically, either because that was the original format or because they have been scanned. The auditor should check that the organization has reviewed the legal admissibility of this storage medium and is complying with any additional requirements for preservation of integrity or availability of these records. The auditor should also check that the organization has considered media deterioration and the accessibility of data if electronic storage media have been chosen, and that the organization has measures in place to ensure the availability of the necessary cryptographic keys, if encryption has been chosen to protect the records.

2.14.1.4 Privacy and protection of personally identifiable information (ISO/IEC 27001:2013, A.18.1.4)

'Privacy and protection of personally identifiable information shall be ensured as required in relevant legislation and regulation where applicable.'

Implementation guidance

In many countries, some legislation or regulation is in place to protect the privacy of personal information. Failure to comply with such legislation can leave the organization open to prosecution and a fine, or at least to serious loss of image and reputation, if it became public. Several laws also specify a number of requirements for the collection, processing, accessibility and protection of personal information on computers. Failure here can also lead to prosecution.

If the organization stores, processes or transmits any personal data, and if there is applicable legislation or regulations, the organization should develop and implement a policy that ensures that no requirements are disregarded. An inventory of personal data assets should be kept, and a role should be given the responsibility for providing guidance to staff and suppliers; responsibility for handling personally identifiable information should be assigned in a manner that complies with legal and contractual requirements. Procedures are necessary to ensure that changes in the use of personal data are reflected as necessary in the asset inventory. A documented review should be carried out at least annually, and compliance with all requirements stated in the relevant laws or regulations should be ensured.

Auditing guidance

Careful control of personally identifiable information is necessary to comply with the applicable legislation and regulations; many countries, for example, in Europe, have data protection legislation. The legislation might also require the organization to register its use of personally identifiable data: the auditor should confirm that the organization has identified all relevant legislative or regulatory requirements, and has put policies, procedures and controls in place to comply with them. The auditor should look also at the type of data held: is it necessary? Has it been validated? Is it transmitted or otherwise conveyed outside the organization? Who has access to this data, and is it necessary for their job function?

The auditor should check that the organization monitors changes to requirements in this area – new, tighter restrictions can be introduced with specified periods for compliance. Is there sufficient awareness within the organization? Are there plans to introduce compliance within the time frame? Auditors should ensure that they themselves are fully up to date with this area of legislation.

2.14.1.5 Regulation of cryptographic controls (ISO/IEC 27001:2013, A.18.1.5)

'Cryptographic controls shall be used in compliance with all relevant agreements, legislation and regulations.'

Implementation guidance

The legal and regulatory requirements and rules for the use of cryptographic controls and the effort and resources necessary to comply with them should be assessed. The results of these assessments should be taken into account in the decision about the use of cryptographic controls. This assessment should include not only the laws and regulations applicable for encryption controls, but also the legal environment for the use of digital signatures and other electronic communications. Because of the differences in the legal situation of various countries, special care should be taken to ensure compliance with legislation in all those countries that are involved in business or travel. ISO/IEC 27002:2013, 18.1.5 lists items that should be taken into account when creating policy and procedures.

Auditing guidance

The organization should present to the auditors the actions it has taken to identify applicable legislation and regulations for cryptographic controls and the legal advice it has taken, where necessary, to ensure compliance. The controls that are taken to fulfil these requirements should be documented, implemented and maintained. The auditor should check that the implementation of the policy for the use of cryptographic controls as described in 2.6.1.1 is commensurate with the legal requirements identified.

2.14.2 Information security reviews (ISO/IEC 27001:2013, A.18.2)

Objective: To ensure that information security is implemented and operated in accordance with the organizational policies and procedures.

2.14.2.1 Independent review of information security (ISO/IEC 27001:2013, A.18.2.1)

'The organization's approach to managing information security and its implementation (i.e. control objectives, controls, policies, processes and procedures for information security) shall be reviewed independently at planned intervals or when significant changes occur.'

Implementation guidance

As with all business activities, the organization's approach to information security and its implementation should be reviewed from time to time to ensure that everything in place is still suitable and effective. The results of the reviews should be reported to management. The review should be carried out by an independent body (either within the organization or outside), to provide assurance to the senior management that the organization's ISMS practices are, indeed, adequate and effective.

'Independent' does not exclude an internal review, provided that the reviewer has appropriate independence from the management and staff being reviewed. An internal audit department would be appropriate. However, a small organization might find it necessary to use an external party for the review. A certification audit undertaken by an accredited organization would also satisfy the requirements of this control.

All results of independent reviews should be recorded, as well as any corrective action that is taken if the independent review identifies areas for improvement.

Auditing guidance

It is important for the auditor to check that independent reviews of the organization's approach to information security and its implementation are taking place, and that they are carried out by an independent party. Without such an independent review, objectivity cannot really be achieved. A third-party audit satisfies the requirement. In cases where third-party audits are not being performed, this requirement can be satisfied by review via internal auditors, management or other bodies external to the security practitioners.

The auditor should check the records of the independent reviews, and should verify that identified corrective actions have been implemented. The results of other reviews, such as those described in 2.1.1.2, should be taken into account.

2.14.2.2 Compliance with security policies and standards (ISO/IEC 27001:2013, A.18.2.2)

'Managers shall regularly review the compliance of information processing and procedures within their area of responsibility with the appropriate security policies, standards and any other security requirements.'

Implementation guidance

If the organization is expending effort and resources in implementing controls, mechanisms should be in place to ensure that these controls are working effectively, as, for example, required by ISO/IEC 27001:2013. Managers should review the compliance with security policies, controls and standards in their area of responsibility. This can take place through a formal review, and/or through spot checks that can occur at any time during normal working hours. A combination of both techniques is possibly most successful.

Managers should react to identified non-compliances as described in control 18.2.2 of ISO/IEC 27002:2013. A documented record of the review should be maintained, noting non-compliances, agreed action and follow-up. The managers should report the results of their reviews into the internal review process (see also 2.14.2.1).

Auditing guidance

In order to determine the degree to which security policies and procedures are being complied with, the auditor should confirm that managers have procedures in place to regularly review this compliance appropriate to their area of responsibility. These reviews should be fully documented, followed up to ensure resolution of non-compliant items, and reported on to the internal review (see also 2.14.2.1), and, as required, to senior management.

Managers should also have procedures in place to react to non-compliances. These procedures should ensure that the reasons for the non-compliances are identified, that any necessary actions are taken to avoid recurrence of the non-compliances, and that the appropriate corrective actions are identified and implemented.

2.14.2.3 Technical compliance review (ISO/IEC 27001:2013, A.18.2.3)

'Information systems shall be regularly reviewed for compliance with the organization's information security policies and standards.'

Implementation guidance

The complexity of information systems, e.g. servers, networks and firewalls, means that with the best intentions they might still be in an insecure state. Organizations may remain vulnerable to attacks and misuse, despite management believing that it has implemented the necessary controls. A full technical review should be carried out at suitable intervals, determined by risk assessment, to detect any technical nonconformities.

Operational information systems require skilled analysis, aided sometimes by special programs that automate certain types of tests. Indeed, the use of such programs allows some tests to be carried out more frequently, as well as more swiftly, and with a lower chance of manual input errors.

These checks should only be carried out by, or under the close supervision of, competent, authorized persons. The integrity and availability of the system could be jeopardized, should an unskilled person attempt this work. In addition, certain types of compliance tests, such as penetration testing, can result in criminal charges (related to computer misuse) if accidentally directed at the wrong systems. Also note that some testing tools may be identified as malware, since their purpose may be to try to compromise a system, and their use by unauthorized users should be treated as an information security incident. Access controls should generally prevent unauthorized persons from carrying out technical compliance reviews (see 2.5.1.1). The installation of tools used for testing should be strictly controlled (also see 2.5.4.5 and 2.8.6.2).

Reviews should be planned and documented; results, nonconformities, actions and follow-up activities should be recorded.

Auditing guidance

The auditor should confirm that the organization has scheduled checks in place to ensure that its information systems conform to security implementation standards. There should be a plan for technical conformity checking, showing what needs to be covered, the frequency and methods employed. It is important that this type of conformity checking is performed by suitably competent and authorized personnel.

If a tool is being used, the auditor should check what aspects of the information systems are actually being reviewed – it could purely be monitoring or it could be conducting an audit of facilities: has it been validated in any way? Check the individuals completing or reviewing the reviews; full compliance can only be assessed by technically competent personnel. Personnel carrying out reviews should also be authorized to do so.

2.12.1.2 Reporting information security events (ISO/IEC 27001:2013, A.16.1.2)

'Information security events shall be reported through appropriate management channels as quickly as possible.'

Implementation guidance

If information security-relevant events occur without being reported and responded to, they might cause more damage than necessary and present a lost opportunity to prevent recurrence. Failure to report events also gives a false sense of security and can compromise risk assessment. Without a reporting procedure, even a major event might not find its way to those responsible for investigation and recovery until serious losses have been experienced. Minor events can be cleared up locally without weakness in control being recognized and corrected.

The definition of an information security event is often difficult in practice, and clear guidance and training are required to ensure that all staff can recognize one when they see it. In plain terms, an information security event is anything that could result in loss or damage to assets, or an action that would be in breach of the organization's security procedures. The organization should consider listing specific reportable events, e.g. a virus detected on a PC or media, suspicion of misuse of a system (possible hacking), theft, password exposure, unexpected results from system monitoring, non-compliance with procedures or controls, uncontrolled system changes, loss of services and human errors. ISO/IEC 27002:2013, 16.1.2 provides a list of categories of information security events.

Any member of staff might be the first to notice a security event; early notification of the event to experienced technical staff can reduce the potential cost related to it by having it investigated quickly. In the case of system abuse, early reporting can significantly reduce the impact of the event. Build a culture of 'no blame' incident reporting – if staff are blamed for their mistakes they will be tempted to cover up the problems. A number of events might already be reportable under the procedures of other departments. Failures of computer and telecommunications equipment, for instance, will be reported to engineers for repair. However, they should also be reported and recorded as information security events (loss of information and service availability). Ensure that there are procedures covering the reporting and investigation of events and that resolving actions are tracked and reported upon.

Reporting procedures should include standardized forms, and guidance upon initial actions to take (or to avoid). Contact points should be documented and staff made aware of them.